Linda is full of energy and great love. She enjoys everything that life has to offer. Being outside enjoying nature, fishing, gardening, playing in the snow like a child, all keeps her plenty happy. She enjoys cooking and baking. She loves people and would do anything to help.

This book is our most Heavenly Father's book to all of you. He used me to write it, but it's guided completely by him to capture the attention of those who need to read this and finally, discover the truth!

I, forevermore, dedicate this book to all the readers. May your life change forever with peace, love, joy, and happiness and may you have the wisdom, strength, courage, and faith needed to obtain this immense love. May your heart, mind, body, spirit, and soul be filled with the holy spirit. May he live inside you and take control of your thoughts, words, actions, and deeds, for this journey of yours be so fabulous that you will be full of joy! May his presence be in you every second of the day and night. Stay filled with God's beautiful blessings! Enjoy and love life!

Linda Fay Black

TRUTH

AUSTIN MACAULEY PUBLISHERS™

LONDON · CAMBRIDGE · NEW YORK · SHARJAH

Ordering Information:
Quantity sales: special discounts are available on quantity purchases by corporations, associations, and others. For details, contact the publisher at the address below.

Publisher's Cataloging-in-Publication data
Black, Linda Fay
Truth

ISBN 9781645362203 (Paperback)
ISBN 9781645362210 (Hardback)
ISBN 9781645368526 (ePub e-book)

Library of Congress Control Number: 2020900685

www.austinmacauley.com/us

First Published (2020)
Austin Macauley Publishers LLC
40 Wall Street, 28th Floor
New York, NY 10005
USA

mail-usa@austinmacauley.com
+1 (646) 5125767

I have so much and so many people to be thankful for. There are so many, I could write a book just on that. I will start with thanking our most amazing Heavenly Father. His sweet, precious son, Jesus. Of course, I must thank the Holy Spirit. I also thank our most beautiful Heavenly Mother, blessed Mother Mary. The sweet angels, saints, and apostles, and heavenly helpers from above.

I would also like to thank my precious husband, Sebastian Black, for how supportive he has been for me and for all he does for me and our family. His belief and love for me has helped so much. When I felt like giving up, he would encourage and help me move forward. I truly thank God for him being in my life.

Our precious daughter, Ayla Duffield, and her husband, Sean, and their beautiful children, Kaelyn Duffield and Jordan Duffield. Their love is unexplainable. I will always hold a special spot in my heart for our daughter, Ayla, and the grandchildren that I am so blessed to have in my life. We are so close, and nothing will separate the love we have. I am very grateful.

Our daughter, Tiffany Jandres, for spending one on one time with me and letting us connect and becoming

so close. She is so beautiful inside and out. Her husband, Joel, and children, Braden, Jamie, and Christian. Our Most loving precious son, Aaron Black, and his son, Colton. He is a true gift from God.

His kind and loving heart is one of a kind. I love being in his presence and having him for a son. Watching him conquer life and be blessed with such a loving heart is inspiring to all who encounter him. Our sweet daughter, Ashley, for finding you Lord and seeing your most pleasant gifts of light, true happiness, peace, joy, and love. Now that she has found you, her life will change for glorious things and blessings to come her way. Watching this and seeing prayers answered has made such an inspiration for me and my journey.

I would like to thank all my friends and family for supporting me with this huge project and giving me the time needed to get this done. I would like to thank my mother-in-law for showing me true love and how kindness and love always work through the hands of Jesus and Mary. Now that I have learned this, I feel inspired to write and show everyone how simple and joyous life can be if you just believe and put your faith and trust in our sweet loving hands from above. I give such a special thank you to my publishing team and others involved with this special book and giving me the confidence I needed to just write. I give a special thanks to my journey-team friends for being a special heavenly family for me and increasing my faith in such a special way.

I thank all my St. James Catholic Church crew for being so supportive and loving.

Thank you all for your kind prayers. I have felt them all the way through. I love you all so much and truly thank you! A special thanks to our priest, Father Jeff, with St. James Catholic Church, and my special Journey crew from Missoula. Everyone in our local community, thank you for your support, friendship, and being such wonderful people. I really love you all. Thank you.

Table of Contents

May all of you be blessed with the
TRUTH

Act love, see love, feel love, show love, speak love
embrace love, and be love.

Chapter 1

Where Am I

I remember just kind of floating around in a very happy place. It looked and felt like the ray outside of the sunshine. Everything was very colorful and beautiful. The colors were like rainbow colors but not in a rainbow appearance. Everything and everyone flowed. Everyone seemed always happy. I felt safe, content, and never wanted to leave. There was laughter and joy surrounding me. This felt so very pleasant. I didn't know anything else. Everything looked and felt like love. There was no sadness or anger, it was all happiness. I don't remember all the details. It was not like Earth at all. There was nothing to worry about because everything was perfect. I couldn't imagine anything better than this.

Suddenly, it was my turn for something exciting to happen. There was so much excitement and cheer. The spirits around me were so excited that it made me feel the same way! I was brought to the center of many spirits. It was like everyone seemed not like the image of people, but more like the image of a spirit. I guess that is what I would call it, for to describe it is difficult. Everyone was white and oval shaped with a glowing, flowing effect. I took a picture of what I feel would describe what I am trying to say. God has been helping me to write this story. It's his story using me, and what I have experienced to tell it. He feels the need for the story to be told and is helping me with this. He gave me a picture to take so everyone could have an image of what I am trying to describe.

This is a picture that is from God. He helped me get the picture that was needed to give you, an insight of what it is I am trying to describe.

He also gave me more pictures that you will see later as you continue. All these spirits, is what I shall call them, were so delightful. They were so excited and happy for me. A female guided me to come with her. The others watched us and cheered happily with a lot of excitement, I was so happy and excited to see what was going to happen to me. I was brought to a large hole that went down a very long way then I was instructed to keep looking down it. A family appeared, she asked me to keep watching so, I continued. It was like watching TV. I had never been through this experience before but seemed to know everything. My wisdom was very clear. I was watching this family, as I watched, they seemed busy. They were all doing things. I was told that this family needs my help; I was showed many things that I would do and would go through.

Some of the things shown to me seemed so difficult. I would even do things that I felt ashamed of and that troubled my heart so deeply. I was indeed encouraged that this was a phase and would pass, the troubling things would pass and there would be happy events again. It seemed that the time doing this would be so short. Everything traveled quickly. I knew that if I did this the rewards would be never ending. Time traveled like the speed of light. I was suddenly told I must go now. "They need you now! You need to hurry up and go now," said the female that was in charge and guiding me.

I said, "WAIT! If I do this, will I be able to come back here again?"

There was a lot of joyful laughter and they reassured me, as they all said "*YES!*" with confidence and joy. I remember saying to myself, "I just need to remember," and I was gone. I was gone, and I don't remember what I was going to remember. What I was going to remember would help make things easier for me to be able to do. This family that was chosen for me had a father, named Hilmer; a mother, named Mary; four sons, named Kevin, Orville, Dale, and Daryl, and one daughter, named Elaine. They also had two miscarriages. They were completely done having any more children. Their minds were set on this. The mother had been taking birth control for quite a few years to reassure this would not happen. It didn't work because it happened!

She became pregnant, unwillingly. She was very afraid. "How could this happen?" the mother said. Her heart was so deeply troubled. She knew that she didn't want any more children and made a decision. She figured the best thing to do would be to have an abortion.

They could not afford another child and were done raising children. The father was a very spiritual man. He had a calming appeal to him. You felt at peace in his presence. He also had a fun personality in a childlike way. The mother, Mary, said to him, "Hilmer, I don't want to have this baby. My body can't bear another child. We already have planned for years not to have any more children. I don't understand how this could happen? We have been using the same method for years and it has worked fine. How could this happen? We have no choice, I will have to get an abortion. We don't need to tell anyone about this."

Hilmer, in a soft-spoken voice, said, "Mary, I understand your worries and concerns. We didn't choose this but you know who did—God. God doesn't make mistakes! He knows our future and we should keep this baby and have it because it's God's will. You need to understand that this must be a miracle. The birth control worked for all these years and suddenly you are pregnant. This must be an act of God. We will have this child and God will provide. Don't worry, we will go through this together and trust God. Jesus will take care of everything for us and everything will be fine. I am here with you through it all! Let's put a smile on our faces and be happy! Let's find out what God is bringing to our lives!"

She still wasn't up for having a baby. She had migraine headaches and struggled with severe back pain. She had hurt her back at a younger age and struggled with it for years. She also was still trying to raise the two children she had at home. Hilmer said, "Let's see what this child will bring! Remove your worries and it's time to trust God. Jesus will be with us, we just need to trust him. Please, Mary, let's have this baby! Please!"

Mary said, "OK, I guess you're right! We better get all the kids together this evening for dinner and tell them the news."

Hilmer embraced Mary in her arms and hugged her for a while, rubbed her back, brushed his hand through her hair and gave her a sweet, kind kiss. He helped her feel more comfort with this huge life change. That evening all their children sat down at the dinner table to be together as a whole family. Hilmer had made phone calls to assure this would happen. He let the older children know that were out of the home that he and their mother had some news to share with them. That evening the siblings found out that they would have a new brother or sister added to the family. All the children were delighted and very happy to find this out. The older children let their mom know that they would help with anything they could do. Daryl the youngest son asked, "Can I pick a name out?"

Hilmer looked at Mary and smiled. She gave him a nod of the head. Hilmer said, "I have a great idea! How about if we let all of you pick out a name together? All of you can choose a name that you all agree on."

Everyone was delighted at this idea and already started saying different names. Oddly, they all seemed to think it was time for a girl! They hoped that it was a girl.

In April of 1969, I was born! I happened to be born on a special day of theirs. It was Hilmer and Mary's wedding anniversary. The special day they shall celebrate for many years to come. They lived in a smaller town near Salem, Oregon. Out of 6 children, I happened to be the only one born in the State of Oregon. The rest of my siblings were born in North Dakota. My siblings were quite a bit older than me, they would help my mother out and help take care of me. Everyone got their chance at this, I believe that I became a new toy for some of them. My older brothers might have got a few dates with me on my hips to impress the girls.

Chapter 2

My Best Friend, Jesus

As I grew into a young child, I developed a strong attachment with my Dad, Hilmer. He was a full-blooded Norwegian man. His father, Gilbert, came from Norway. Hilmer was tall, dark-haired, a bit of olive colored skin, big brown eyes and was very handsome. He was slender with long legs. Sometimes he would wear pants that were a bit too short for him. He would wear them anyway. He seemed to dress up a lot and not wear jeans so much. I spent a lot of time hanging around with him. He was so smart and taught me all kinds of stuff. I loved learning things, it was fun! He was also so funny. On a more serious but pleasant note, he would talk to me a lot about Jesus. I grew up Lutheran, our family took Sundays very seriously. We would go to church and after church, we would keep the day a Sabbath day. Sundays were always a special day to enjoy the family and spend time with each other. After church, we would go for a drive together. Sometimes we would walk with my dad and help him find rocks and agates for his collection. We would also go eat in a restaurant and make sure Mom had the day off from cooking and cleaning. My dad was a businessman who loved being around people. He just loved people. He was a gentle man full of love and humor. People were drawn to him like a magnet. My mother was German and Norwegian. Her father Selmer was Norwegian and her mother Elnora was German. She had blonde hair and more of a greenish blue eye color. Her figure was full but not heavy or overweight, just healthy looking. She was very musical. She loved playing the accordion, and the organ. She enjoyed singing, dancing, and entertaining. When she would start playing music, everyone had fun! We all enjoyed it so much! They were very fun people. Sundays were always so much fun! We all loved our family times! Some days were harder and less fun. When my mom would suffer with a migraine, we would let her rest and stay outside, so; the house would remain quiet. I would spend a lot of time playing alone with Jesus. Jesus was my friend. I loved him so much he was with me all the time. My brothers would tease me that I had a crush on Jesus.

Of course, I did not! I did however admire his beauty and friendship I had developed with him. Everything I did, he did with me. Even eating and sleeping. Jesus and I, my very best friend! We talked, sang, laughed, and played. I always felt safe, peaceful, and happy with him. My love for him was huge! I could always just be me with Jesus, and it was OK. When around anyone else, I was extremely shy. With Jesus, I became alive and full of joy! Jesus and I spent a lot of time together. As Jesus spent time with me, he watched me as I grew bigger and older. I became old enough where I had to start school. I was going to be in kindergarten, I was really scared and didn't want to do this at all. I liked it just the way things were. Daryl and Dale would go to school, Dad would go to work, and Mom would let me play with Jesus all day. Now my life would change. My dad knew that I was afraid. He talked to me in such a soothing tone.

Hilmer said, "Linda, I know you're scared about starting school, but I can help you."

I said, "How?"

Hilmer said, "Come with me."

I followed Dad to his office in our house. He had a beautiful writing desk in there. Dad opened a drawer full of beautiful rocks and agates. He picked one out.

Hilmer said, "Hold this rock in your hand and rub it for a minute." Then he asked, "What does the rock feel like?"

I said, "Smooth and soft."

He said, "I am going to show you a trick. You need to put your rock in your pocket. Leave it there. Whenever you feel scared or nervous, just rub your rock and those feelings will go away. You are the only one, well," he laughed, "besides me, that will know it's there. People won't even know that you are rubbing it. It's like a secret. Linda, I still get scared sometimes, but I just rub my rock." He pulled out a rock from his pocket.

He said, "See, I have a rock in my pocket too. I have been using it for years! It always works!"

I said, "Dad, can we trade and I could have yours and you could have mine?"

He smiled, laughed lightly, and he said, "Sure and would you like to pick one out for your teacher?"

I said, "Yes! I will pick out a pretty one for her. I bet she will love it!"

Hilmer smiled and said, "I bet she will too."

"Dad, if I could bring my friend along to school?"

He asked, "Who?"

I said, "Jesus."

He smiled at me so big I thought he was going to laugh but he didn't. Instead, he gave me a huge hug and a kiss on the forehead. He said, "Of course, you can! Linda, Jesus can go with you anywhere and everywhere."

My dad brought Jesus and I to school. Dad put Jesus in the back seat and me up front. When we arrived at the school, my dad had one of my hands and Jesus had the other one. We all walked in together.

I gave my teacher her rock. She said, "Thank you so much! I absolutely love it! That was really sweet of you to think of me and bring me a gift. I look forward to having you in my classroom." She showed me where my desk was. I let her know that I needed another desk by me, for my friend Jesus. The teacher looked at my dad very puzzled.

My Dad smiled and said, "Some kids have imaginary friends, my daughter has Jesus for hers."

My teacher laughed and put a desk by me, I didn't understand why she laughed but was happy she gave Jesus a desk.

She said, "Here is your desk and one for your friend Jesus too! Thank you for bringing a friend with you. I will let him join us for class today and we can all be thankful he is here with us. How does that sound?"

I said, "OK, that would be fine and thank you for letting him be with us today."

My dad gave me a big hug and kiss on the forehead as he said, "Goodbye and have fun! I will see you when school gets out."

I hugged him back. I really wanted him to stay and started feeling scared! *Oh! Rub my rock.* I realized I had my rock and my best buddy was right next to me. *I will be safe and brave!* I held my rock in my hand and rubbed it. I loved how smooth and silky it felt and it was very soothing. My dad was right! It worked and definitely calmed me. Now I was ready for this new experience and to learn things. When it came to play time, I decided that I would just play with Jesus. My teacher allowed that, but the other children just laughed at me. When it came to Jesus and me, I sure got laughed at a lot. I ignored them and played with Jesus anyway. One girl walked up to me and said, "You are weird! I don't see anyone sitting in the desk next to you!" She made me feel sad so I put my head down and ignored her while I rubbed my rock some more. I looked up at her as she stared at me. My teacher came over and said, "Let's all be nice to each other and please use kind words. Linda's friend is just here for today and even though you may not see him, we still need to be nice and respectful." The girl said, "OK and I'm sorry." She walked away with her head down looking at the floor. Jesus and I drew and colored butterflies together. We had so much fun! Before I knew it, it was time to go home. My dad arrived and gave me a big hug. He talked to the teacher for a moment. We gathered my things, got in Dad's mercury, and drove home. Jesus was in the back seat and I was up front with Dad. As Dad was driving us home, he said, "Linda, what did you learn at school today?"

I said, "I learned that people are mean!" He asked, "Why?" I said, "Because they are mean to my friend Jesus, but he still loves them anyway."

He said, "Oh, Linda! It's OK, they just don't see your friend like you do. They must get to know him like you and then they will be his friend too."

I said, "But Dad, I didn't have to get to know him, I already knew him before I came down here!"

He looked at me weird and said, "What do you mean?"

I pointed up and said, "When I was up there."

Dad said, "What were you doing up there?"

I said, "I guess I was having a lot of fun! And everything was just really nice and happy."

He said, "Why did you come down here?"

I said, "Because they made me to help a family."

Dad said, "Is that family us?"

I said, "Yep!"

He said, "What do you have to do to help us?"

I told him, "Well, a lot of things were shown to me. It was like watching TV so a lot of different things were happening and I'm not sure what help I am, but I will have to go through lots of stuff and it won't take long to do and then I can go back. They said I could come back there. I was trying to remember something really important but I can't remember what it was. They sent me here so fast I forgot what it was."

Dad asked if I could describe what I saw up there. I told him, "I don't know how, it was colorful like the colors in a rainbow but all over and I knew everything already. You will just have to see when you get there. You will love being there."

He said, "Linda, this is something you shouldn't tell people, it will just be our secret, OK?"

I asked, "Why, Dad?"

He said, "People will act different and they won't understand. People might try and tease you or make fun of you so we will just keep it as our secret, OK?"

I said, "OK."

He said, "If you want to talk more about it or remember more, I would love it if you talk to me about it though because I do understand, sweetheart."

I said, "I know that I didn't have all these feelings I have now because everything was always perfect! I didn't have to feel like this."

He said, "How do you feel?"

I said, "I feel sad and like crying."

He asked, "Why, honey?"

I said, "Because people don't care about what they say to anyone."

Dad said, "Honey, people care. We all have feelings and get our feelings hurt. Some people just haven't learned to be kind yet, but they will. What about this?" As he tickled me under my arm, I started to giggle and he said, "How does that make you feel?" I laughed! From that day forward, I never talked to anyone about it again. It was my secret with Dad. Dad always knew how to brighten my day and make me feel happy.

When we got home, I was starving, and Mom just pulled fresh bread out of the oven. My mouth was watering, I couldn't wait to have a piece! My dad and I both sat down and ate a piece. Every bite was savory, and I had extra butter on mine, dripping. This is so good, Mom! You are the best cook in the whole world. Dad agreed and gave Mom a big hug and kiss and then me. He had to get back to work. I asked my mom if I could have two more pieces of bread.

She said, "No, have one and after you eat that, I will give you another one." I started crying. She couldn't understand why I was behaving like this. I told her, "Mom, I want my friend to have a piece too! Please! I always share with him! Please Mom!"

She asked me, "What friend, Linda? It's just you and I here. Nobody else is here!"

I said, "No! My friend Jesus is here too! Why is everyone so mean to him?"

She gave me an odd look, gave me a hug, and said, "It's OK, I will give you two."

"I was so happy!" I said, "Thank you, Mom, you make the best bread! Jesus is going to love this!"

She smiled and said, "Well, if Jesus doesn't want it, bring it back."

"Oh, don't worry, Mom. Jesus will want this." I went out by my tree and shared my bread with Jesus. He was so happy and loved it! I knew that he would.

Soon after my brothers arrived and started to tease me. "What are you doing? Playing with Jesus again?" They started laughing and went inside.

I told Jesus that I was so sorry that they do this. I said, "They just don't know you like I do."

My sister was deaf, so she went to a deaf school. I hardly saw much of her. Her name was Elaine. She was very pretty but she talked different than us. Sometimes people laughed at her too, just like Jesus and me. My oldest brother Kevin had his own house but would still stop in and visit us. He would usually have some of his friends with him. They were all very nice. My second oldest brother Orville had his own place too. He would still come see us. He was my favorite brother. He would come driving up in his cool car called an MGB and ask me to come for a ride with him and we would go to the candy store. I would run as fast as I could, kicking my heals to my butt to get in his car! This was a little car, so Jesus would wait for me to get back. On the way to the candy store, Orville asked me how school was.

I told him, "Good! Dad gave me an agate to give to my teacher and he let me take Jesus with me."

He smiled at me and said, "I am happy for you and I bet Jesus enjoyed the day with you in school."

"Yep! He gets to come with me every day."

He smiled and said, "That's good!" He asked me if I made lots of new friends.

I said, "Nope, I didn't need to. I already have a friend."

He said, "It's OK, Linda, you can have other friends too. I'm sure Jesus would like that too."

I said, "Maybe, we will see, but they better be nice to Jesus if they want to be my friend."

Orville started laughing and said, "Oh, OK!"

I didn't understand why he thought that was so funny, but it didn't matter because we were going to get candy! We saw a car full of women and they waved at my brother to pull over in a parking lot, so they could talk. In the parking lot they pulled up next to us. Orville said, "Hi, this is my little sister, Linda. We're out cruising and going to the candy store." They all stared at me, so I looked down at the floor.

Orville said, "She is shy."

One of them said, "Oh, she is sweet, how adorable." My face was boiling hot. One of the women got out of the car and came up to Orville and asked if he liked her tan line.

She pulled her shirt down by her shoulder and showed him. She was very pretty.

Orville said, "You look beautiful, the tan is great! Would you like to meet up with me later and we could go do something?"

She said, "Yes, that would be great!" and gave him her phone number. She said, "Bye, Linda, it was nice meeting you."

I waved bye at her and Orville said, "I will call you in a bit."

She said, "Sounds good!" We left and soon arrived at the candy store. I couldn't wait I was so excited! I loved candy! There was so much candy, it was hard to pick which one I wanted. Orville told me to hurry up and that I could go ahead and pick three. I said OK. I thought I was going to only choose one so this made me happy and made me hurry before he changed his mind. I finally figured it out. I got some red licorice, a package of candy called Zott's cherry flavored and a recess peanut butter cup. We headed home. When we arrived home, I gave my brother a hug and said thank you. I grabbed my bag of candy and started to head to my tree. Orville asked me what I was doing. I said I am going to share my candy with Jesus.

He said, "Oh, OK. Well, have fun and tell Jesus hi from me." Before eating our candy, my dad always taught us to pray before eating, so we did. After we got done eating, we talked, played, and sang songs together as usual. I told Jesus about the girl with the tan line. It was a fantastic day! Soon my dad pulled into the driveway. I was so happy to see him! I went running up to him and gave him a huge hug! He always had the biggest brightest smile and would bend down by me, so we could be face-to-face and eye-to-eye. He would always take time with me and visit, play a little, and make me giggle before going in the house. I loved playing with my dad. He was so much fun! I decided I wanted to go inside and hang out with Dad some more. When I got in the house, it smelled so good.

I said, "Dinner smells good, Mom!"

She said, "I hope everyone enjoys it!"

I said, "By the smell of it, I sure will!"

My dad was watching TV and sitting on his recliner. I climbed up on his lap and cuddled with him. I loved cuddling with my dad and he always smelled so good. I would sneak sniffs of him.

He asked, "Would you like to watch the Flintstones?"

I said, "Sure I would." We watched the Flintstones together as we cuddled. I felt so happy, content, and comfortable. Soon my brothers arrived. After they cleaned up, it was time to eat. We gathered at the table together in our spots. We prayed, dished up, and began eating. My dad wanted to know how everyone's day went.

We talked and soon Dad said, "I have some news to tell you Linda. Tomorrow, I can take you to school, but I will not be able to pick you up." He said a woman would be picking me up and taking me to her house where there would be more children. After Dale and Daryl get out of school, they would pick me up and bring me home. I would only be there for a short while. My mom couldn't come get me because we only had one car. I felt scared and worried. He could tell somehow. He soothed me and let me know that I would be OK. Not to worry. I asked if I could bring Jesus with me. He smiled and said, "Absolutely, you can!"

My brothers laughed, and my mother smiled. Dad told Dale and Daryl to stop laughing as it was not nice! I looked at both and glared! Dad told me, "Linda, be nice!"

The next day it was time for Dad to bring me to school again. Dad, Jesus, and I were off again! When we arrived, we, all held hands while walking into the school together. When we got to the classroom, I saw that there was no desk for Jesus. I asked the teacher where his desk was. She said, "Oh, I wasn't sure if he would be with you today."

"He will be with me every day because he likes to learn too."

She said, "OK, now that I know this, I will make sure his desk stays by yours." I smiled at her and said thank you.

Jesus and I got situated. My dad talked to the teacher for a minute and reminded me about the lady picking me up. He said, "The teacher knows."

I told him, "Make sure the lady knows about Jesus, so she will have room for him in her vehicle."

He smiled and hugged me and said, "I already let her know," and winked at my teacher. I had a terrific day in school and listened to my brother Orville about playing with the other kids. I played with them and they played with Jesus too. We all played together and had so much fun! I loved this day! It was perfect! I was so happy that my new friends didn't laugh at me and played with Jesus too. Jesus really liked this too! It was my best day ever!

Chapter 3

My Good Day Went Bad

Soon this lady came and picked Jesus and I up. There were other kids she picked up as well. Nobody got introduced, we were just told to get in the car. She seemed eager to get going and kind of grumpy. She brought us to her house. The house was a large two story, older looking home. There was a smaller front yard with a tree on the corner of the sidewalk. The paint was starting to come off and the stairs going to the house had a wooden deck to the entrance. When we first walked in, there was a large dining room table where the other kids knew to sit down. She gave us peanut butter and jelly sandwiches. This man came into the room. I felt very afraid of him so hid under the table with Jesus. The tablecloth was long enough that he could not see me.

He made the other kids go in a different room with him. I could hear a girl crying and telling him, "Please, stop." He got angry and told the other kids, "None of you better ever tell anybody or if you do, I will kill your families." I was so scared, my heart was thumping so loud and fast that I could hear it. I was trying so hard not to make any noise. I could hear myself breathing very hard.

Jesus took my hand and said, "Linda, come with me."

We went out the front door together and he brought me to a hiding spot by a tree. He said we needed to be very quiet. He told me to stay with him and he would keep me safe. He said, "Do not go back in that house ever again, it is too dangerous."

I asked him, "How will my brothers know where to find me?"

Suddenly, I smelled the smell of beautiful flowers and such a sweet pleasant smell. He told me, "Do not worry, I will make sure your brothers see you." Then I felt safe and soothed! I knew that I could trust Jesus! He hugged me and let me know that he was with me and would never ever leave me. He said, "I am always with you everywhere." I noticed a big pile of ants by us and almost screamed! Jesus stopped me and said, "It's OK, they cannot hurt you. It is OK, just watch them and let them be." As I watched them, it was very interesting how hard they worked and how they helped each other. Jesus was right, they wouldn't hurt me. They seemed nice. Soon I could hear my brothers talking. I went running up to them and said, "Please, take me home now, I never ever want to come back here again." Daryl bent down to me and asked, "What happened? Why are you out here by yourself?"

I said, "I'm not, I am with Jesus! Please let's go now, we must hurry and get out of here!"

I started to run. Daryl ran after me and said, "Stop. What happened? You need to tell me."

I started crying hard and told him, "I can't. I can't ever tell anyone. Please stop asking me and let's hurry."

He grabbed me and gave me a hug. He said, "It's OK, Linda, we will bring you home." He told Dale, "Come on, let's just take her home." When we got home, Daryl asked me to stay outside and play with Jesus for a while.

I said, "OK."

After a while my mom came over to me. She said, "Linda, what happened at that house today?"

I started to cry hard. I told her, "Mom, I can't tell you. You don't understand, I can't tell anyone." I got angry and said, "I wish everyone would just stop asking me what happened and leave me alone!"

She grabbed me and hugged me and said, "I am sorry." She asked, "Can you just tell me, did anyone hurt you?"

I said, "No, Mom, Jesus took me outside and we hid until Daryl and Dale came." She sighed with relief and told me that I did the right thing and that she was so glad that Jesus helped me. I said, "Me too!"

Soon, Dad came pulling up in the driveway very fast and came running up to us. My mom stopped him and said, "She is OK. Don't ask her any more questions. It's already been a hard-enough day for her." My dad picked me up and held me for a long time. He promised that I would never have to go back there again. He put me down, gave me a kiss on the forehead. He gave my mom a big hug and kiss and said, "I better get back to work, but we can talk more later. Keep a close eye on her!"

Mom said, "I will!" I just wanted to forget everything and never think about it again! I asked if I could stay outside and play with Jesus.

Mom said, "Yes, I think that's a wonderful idea."

My brothers kept coming and checking on me to see if I was OK. They treated me much nicer than normal and kept on wanting hugs. That was nice of them, but it was starting to get annoying and interrupting my playtime with Jesus. I was still nice to them because they were acting like they loved me. Soon my dad came pulling up in the driveway. He got out of the car and I went running up to him as usual. He lifted me up high in the air! He kept kissing my face and telling me how much he loved me. I kept giggling because his kisses tickled. My dad was tall, thin, dark-haired, with big brown eyes. He was so handsome that I just loved looking at him and studying his face. I knew every part of my dad's face! Between my dad, Mom, Jesus, and my brothers, I felt very safe and loved. We went inside. Dad said hi to everyone. He gave my mom a hug and a kiss, with me on his hip as he carried me around with him. We went to the recliner and cuddled while watching the Flintstones. My day seemed all better.

That evening while I was sleeping, I had a horrible nightmare. I could hear that girl crying and that mean man was coming after me. I was terrified! I got up and went into my parent's room. I was trying to be very quiet and not wake them up. I squeezed in by my dad and lay next to him. He put his arm around me and covered me up with the blanket. He said, "It's OK, go to sleep."

The next morning, it was time to get up and get ready for school. I did and soon Dad told me to say goodbye to everyone. Then it was time to leave so we did the usual, put Jesus in the back seat first and then I up front with Dad. On the way to school, Dad asked me why I came and slept by him? I told him that I had a very bad dream. He asked, "What was your dream about?"

I said, "Dad, I really don't feel like talking about it if that's OK."

He asked, "Was it about what happened at that house? It's OK, you don't have to talk about it." He reassured me that I was safe now, and he would keep me safe and make sure that nothing ever happens to me.

I said, "OK, let's talk about something else."

He took my hand and drove with one hand on the steering wheel and the other holding mine all the way to school. When we got to school, he let Jesus out and then me. We all held hands as we walked into the school. When we got in the classroom, Jesus' desk was right by mine. My teacher put things on his desk like everyone else got.

That was so nice of her. She would smile at me as she did. I really liked her. Again, I had a wonderful day at school. My new friends played with Jesus and I and we all had fun. Dad came and got us and took us home. For quite some time, I kept having nightmares. I would go sleep by Dad every night. One day Dad came home from work and had some exciting news. At the dinner table he let all of us know that we would be moving back to North Dakota. I had never been there before, but the rest of the family had. He got a new job opportunity to make more money.

Everyone seemed fine with this. I asked if Jesus could come with us too.

He said, "Of course, we wouldn't have it any other way." Nobody laughed this time. He told my mom that his work had a house that was bigger than the one we have now that we could move into. He said you will also be able to have a garden and flowers. She was excited and happy. He said that he would drive the U-Haul and Dale could help Mom drive the car with everyone. I asked if Jesus and I could please ride in the U-Haul with him.

He said, "Yes, I figured on that already." I was so excited! This would be so fun! He let us know that this would be a long drive and that we needed to start packing.

Chapter 4

A Good Move

We all pitched in and helped pack everything in our home. My brother's helped Mom wrap stuff and put it into boxes. Everyone was busy. Jesus and I packed all my stuffed animals and toys. My brothers helped carry all the boxes and furniture and put it in the U-Haul. After we got everything out of the house, it was time for us to load up and go. Jesus sat between my dad and me. This was a huge truck and we sat very high. We could see everything. This was so fun, I loved it! Dad, Jesus, and I talked, sang, laughed, and Dad told us all kinds of stories about the land and things we saw. He was super smart! My Dad knew everything! We would stop to get gas, use the restroom, and eat. It seemed like it took forever to get to our new house, but we finally arrived. We all went inside. We picked our bedrooms out and Mom fell in love with her new kitchen. We had a huge yard, much bigger than our other place. I couldn't wait to get my bedroom ready and go play in our huge yard with Jesus. This was perfect! Our house was much bigger and nicer. I was full of joy! Jesus really liked our new home too! This was the best home ever! We got everything unloaded, unpacked, and put away. Now our home looked like our family home. Mom did a good job of decorating. She was singing with joy the whole time. Mom sang so pretty. I loved listening to her sing. We were all very tired. When I went to bed in my new bedroom, I made a spot on my bed for Jesus and my favorite stuffed animals that I called stuffies.

My dad read me a story. My mom came in the room and listened to Dad read to us. We said our goodnight prayers and they tucked me in and gave me hugs and kisses goodnight. I slept so well! I didn't even have any bad dreams. I was so excited to go play in our new yard with Jesus! It was time to explore! My dad told me that I couldn't because I had to start my new day at school. He would bring me today and then I would ride the bus. I was super excited to ride the bus! I had never been on a bus before. I was feeling scared to start a new school. I just got comfortable at my old one. Dad wanted to know what was wrong. Dad could always tell when something was bothering me. I talked to him about how I was feeling.

He told me, "You have no need to worry. I already talked to your teacher, Linda. She is so nice, you are going to really like her. She is short on desks though, so Jesus will have to share with you. She is very excited to meet you and happy that you and Jesus will be in her class."

I said, "Do you think the other kids will laugh at me?"

Dad said, "Oh no! They will be so happy to have a new friend." He wanted to know why I thought they would laugh at me.

I said, "Everyone always does when they find out that Jesus is my friend."

He said, "Oh, don't worry, sweet heart, nobody will laugh at you! They just wish Jesus could be their friend too! You will have to teach them how he can."

I said, "Yep! Jesus loves everybody, Dad!"

He smiled and said, "You can let them know that." I asked if I could bring my teacher an agate.

He said, "OK, but we must hurry, we don't want to be late."

I picked out a round one with black and brown spots. It was smooth and shiny. My dad gave me another one to put in my pocket.

I said, "Thank you, Dad, now I have two."

He said, "You're welcome. Let's go so we are not late."

Dad, Jesus, and I were on our way. Soon we arrived at the school. It was much smaller than my other school. Dad and Jesus held my hands as we walked in the school together. We went to the front desk. My dad filled out paperwork and the lady told us where my classroom was. She was very nice. We all held hands and walked to the classroom together. The teacher was very pretty. I gave her the agate. She thought it was so beautiful and thanked me. I let her know that if she ever gets scared, she can rub it and she won't be afraid anymore. She said, "I will save it forever." She told my dad that he is lucky to have such a sweet girl and smiled at me. She asked if she could have my hand and she would show me where to sit. I said, "Sure" and gave her my hand. Her hand felt soft. My dad gave me a hug and told me that the teacher would help me get on the bus after school. He said to have a terrific day and smiled and winked at the teacher and said goodbye. After dad left, the teacher took my hand again and had me stand up in front of the class. She introduced me to everyone and had each student stand up and tell me what their names were. There weren't many kids in the class. It was much smaller than my other class. That was kind of nice in a way. It made me feel better.

The teacher said, "The chair next to Linda is our new friend Jesus. You can't see him, but he is there. Everyone, say Hi to Jesus and wave at him." They each did that, and nobody laughed. All these kids were much nicer than the ones at my other school. She wanted all the kids to tell something that they enjoy doing. She asked me to do the same.

I said, "I enjoy eating candy, going to church, listening to my dad's stories, and playing with Jesus. I sometimes enjoy spending time with my brothers. They tickle me and play with me too. I love listening to my mom sing and play music and eating her yummy food." The teacher asked everyone to say hi to me and wave at me. I said "Hi" and waved at all of them.

She said, "You may sit down now, Linda, and everyone else can sit back down too."

It was a super fun day! Even though there weren't very many kids, they all played with Jesus and me and were very nice. Some of them already knew Jesus but just had never played with him before. I had so much fun and I loved my new teacher and my new school. It was the best day ever!

After school, my teacher grabbed my hand and walked me to the bus to ride home. She said, "I am so proud of you, Linda, and happy to have you in my class. Linda, you are an angel! You're like a breath of fresh air! Exactly what our classroom needed!"

Daryl and Dale were standing by the bus waiting for me. The teacher introduced herself to them and said, "Linda fit in well and had a good day. The whole class really likes her and so do I," as she smiled at me. She said, "You guys are lucky to have this girl for your sister." Daryl and Dale thanked her, and we got on the bus. The bus was so fun! We sat in back and when we would go over bumps, my butt would raise in the air. We would all laugh and wait for the next one. When we got home, I was very hungry! I ran in the house and Mom had the house smelling good like she always did. Mom wanted to know how school was.

I told her that I loved it and the bus was super fun!

She said, "I am happy for you! Are you hungry?"

I said, "Yep."

She gave me two homemade chocolate chip cookies and a glass of milk. She said you and Jesus can each have a cookie, but you will have to share the milk.

I gave her a big hug and said, "Thanks, Mom!"

We lived out in the Country and there was a Grain Elevator close to our house. This is where my dad worked. My mom asked me if I would like to bring some cookies to Dad. I said, "Sure." She put some in a bag and told me to go up the stairs on the side of the building and that is where my dad's office would be. I said OK and Jesus and I headed out. There were railroad tracks close to the elevator. We went up the stairs and opened the door. My dad was sitting down at a desk talking to some men. They were all laughing because my dad was telling Ole and Lena jokes. They were my dad's favorite jokes to tell. Dad said Hi to me and introduced me to everyone. One of the guys wanted to know if he could buy me a pop. Dad let him. I got an orange crush from the pop machine in Dad's office.

I told the man thank you. I gave Dad his cookies and he said, "Thank you! How was school?"

I said, "Fantastic! I love my new school." He put a chair by him and told me to sit down. He gave me some paper and some colors and said I could color him a picture to put on the wall. Jesus and I started to color our usual beautiful butterflies. Dad continued to tell jokes and have fun with the guys. It seemed like Dad really liked his new job and that the people sure liked him. It was fun listening to them laugh and have fun. After we got done with our picture for Dad, he hung it up on the wall.

He said, "You better make some more because this place needs some art." I smiled and started to color some more.

One of the other guys said, "You sure are doing a good job and you color very nice."

I said, "Yep! That's because Jesus is helping me."

They looked at me and smiled but didn't laugh. The people around here were sure nice. I ended up having so much fun with Dad and his new friends that I forgot about playing outside and exploring. Soon it was time for Dad and me to walk home. On the way home, Dad took me to a lilac bush. He said it was his most favorite smell and had me smell it. It really did smell good and they were very pretty too.

I asked, "Can we pick some to give to Mom?" My dad thought that was a fantastic idea. We picked a big bundle. Jesus helped us. When we got home, Mom had dinner ready and we gave her the flowers. She was so surprised and so happy.

She gave us both a hug and kiss. I loved my mom's smile. Dad told her that the flowers weren't near as beautiful as she was. She smiled at him and started to turn a little red in the face. That happened to me sometimes too. After dinner, I asked if I could go play outside for a while. Jesus and I went outside and started exploring. We found all kinds of neat things and a big tree that we could do our coloring by too. We loved this place. Soon my brothers arrived. They seemed happier and nicer than usual.

I asked them, "Do you guys like our new home?"

They both said yes. Dale said, "And the girls are cuter here too." They both laughed. They wanted to know if I wanted them to twirl me, I did as that's my favorite! They took turns, holding my hands and running around in circles until I would fly up in the air like a bird.

Sometimes they would need a break and I guess I did too because I would feel dizzy and wouldn't walk very good. We would all laugh. It felt funny and looked funny too. They would hold me on the ground and tickle torture me.

I liked it and hated it at the same time but couldn't help myself from laughing. We stayed living here for quite a long time. I never had any more bad dreams. My horrible, terrifying experience was vanished and not talked about again.

Chapter 5
Drugs Are Bad

After a few years went by, it was time to move again for a different job opportunity for Dad. We have done this before, so we all knew what we had to do. This time we moved to a town. Our house was close to the Elevator again, so Dad could walk to work. Sometimes he would drive though. We adjusted to everything new again. I still held on to my special relationship with Jesus but being older, I talked of him less. I learned that if I spoke the truth, people would think I was weird when I talked about Jesus. I just stopped talking about him around people but still knew he was always with me. He knew it wasn't me, that it was them, so he wasn't upset with me and understood. He wanted me to be happy. I met lots of new friends and started playing every day with a few of them. I had one friend that I loved playing with all the time. He was a boy, so my brothers always teased me that he was my boyfriend. I would get so mad at them because it wasn't true. He was just my friend. My buddy! I still liked hanging out with my dad too. Nothing would ever change that! After some time had passed, I noticed great changes in my older brother Dale.

He was acting so different and very moody. Daryl and I would talk about it and we were concerned about his behavior. His bedroom was in the basement. He had a big bedroom. When he was home, he would spend a lot of time in his room instead of with us. He would say he already ate and that he wasn't hungry. Dale would spend a lot of time with his friends and sometimes he wouldn't even come home. He would get in horrible fights with my dad and was so mean to him. I felt bad for Dad. One evening he even threw a watch at Dad. My Mom and Dad were starting to argue too. Mom would always try and stand up for Dale and Dad didn't like that. Daryl and I didn't like that neither. Dad wasn't doing anything wrong. Dale was the one being ridiculous. I never saw my parents argue before all this started happening. It appeared our family was falling apart and everyone was walking around on eggshells around Dale. Daryl and I both tried talking to Dale, but it didn't do any good. Finally, my dad got so upset with Dale that he started investigating what was going on. He found out that Dale and his friends were doing cocaine, marijuana, and drinking a lot. Dale's grades were falling, and he wasn't a track star anymore. My dad decided the only way to fix this mess was for all of us to go to Minot North Dakota for a family treatment program. It would get Dale sober and help all of us be counseled on how to cope with this as a family. It seemed like forever that we stayed in Minot and did this, but truthfully, I am not sure how long we really were there.

After this was over, we learned a lot of things and our family was back to normal and much better. By going through all this, my brother Daryl and I talked and decided that we would never have anything to do with drugs. Drugs were bad and caused a lot of bad things to happen. We were both scared to death of drugs. We witnessed and saw the effect it did. Dad did the right thing and fixed everything. Dad was good at fixing things. I loved him so much and forever thankful to have him for a dad.

Chapter 6
An Everlasting Life Change

After some time had passed, Dad had another announcement to make at the dinner table. He said that we would be moving again. This time it wouldn't be too far away. He had bought a restaurant. He and Mom would run it, and we would all help and work there too. We would get paid for working. It would be a family business and the name of the restaurant would be called "Mary's Diner." He had a house lined up right by the school that I would attend, and it would be by far the nicest house that we ever lived in. He said, "This would be a good change for all of us and we need to move forward with life and always improve things. Mom likes to cook and does a good job at it. I am good at business management, and you would all make great employees. Everyone can make money in our family instead of just me."

This was exciting news, but I was kind of sad to leave my friends and school. It was OK though, I trusted my dad and really wanted my brother Dale to find new friends. We all were willing to do what it took to keep this family together. Soon it was time to pack and load the U-Haul again. Exactly like last time. My brothers with Mom, and

Jesus and I with Dad. It didn't take long at all to arrive at our new home. My school was very close to our house. Our house was enormous. It seemed like it was compared to the other homes we lived in. Here is a picture of it taken in 2018. It still is there and so is the school. Here is a picture of the house and of the school.

Our New House

The School

We all went inside. Dad was right! This way by far the most beautiful home that we had ever lived in. It was so big I couldn't believe it! We each picked out our bedrooms and then Dad had us get in the car, so we could go see our restaurant. This was so neat! I was super excited! Everyone seemed to be just as excited as me. My mom was smiling from ear to ear. My mom loved cooking, and this would give her and Dad a chance to do something together. My mom was such a good cook, we knew all the people that would come to eat here would love Mom's food. Everything she made always tasted good. They both enjoyed people and got along with people well. I thought this was going to be very enjoyable for all of us. I was excited to make my own money and my brothers were too. We went back to the house and started unloading, unpacking, and putting things away.

We did this before, so we had a system that worked. We made a good team. By the time we got everything done, we were all very tired. We were all exhausted! I had a spot for Jesus and my stuffies on my bed.

Mom and Dad tucked me in and we said our goodnight prayers. I think I fell asleep before I finished praying.

When I woke up, I was so excited, I went running into Mom and Dad's room. I jumped up on the bed and sat between them. I said, "Good Morning!"

They hugged me and tickled me.

Dad said, "I sure am glad that you are so happy! We have a lot to do today and we are going to need your help. Can you help us today?"

I asked him if I would start getting paid today. He laughed and said, "You sure will."

I said, "Sure, I will help you. Anything you need me to do I will do!"

He smiled and said, "OK, let's go get your sleepy head brothers up!"

I giggled! Dad carried me up the stairs to wake them. We woke them up and Dad said, "Hurry up and get ready because we have lots to do today."

I said, "We start getting paid to work today!"

They said "OK" and that they would get dressed and be right down. We had a bathroom upstairs too, so that was nice for all of us not to have to share one bathroom. We had three bathrooms in this house. It sure was a nice house! When we got downstairs, Mom already had breakfast made. Boy! She was fast! She was like magic! We all sat down and ate. After we were done eating, Mom told Dad that she would clean up and then meet us at the restaurant. She would help us when she got there.

Dad said, "OK, no problem. We will go get started!" I got to sit up front and Jesus sat between Daryl and Dale.

I didn't care what anyone thought! My life was so much better when Jesus was included in everything! That's just what I knew! If people didn't like me talking about him then they didn't have to! That was just going to have to be their problem, not mine. When we arrived at the restaurant, Dad had the key to unlock the doors and let us in. Dad gave us each a bunch of chores to do.

He said that he needed to go home to make a lot of phone calls and order supplies and such. Dad let us know that the more we got done, the more we would be paid, and the less we would have to do this evening. We said "OK" and got busy. By the time Dad got back, we had the place shining and smelling nice and fresh. We cleaned everything spotless! Mom was helping us too. She was cleaning the kitchen while we cleaned the rest of the building. The kitchen was enormous, so she had a lot of work to do. I knew that Dad would be so proud of all of us! Dad could not believe what a wonderful job we all did!

He said, "I knew I could count on all of you! Great job, gang! The place almost looks ready to open!"

My brothers were talking about what they were going to do with their money. Daryl asked, "What are you going to do with your money, Linda?"

Dale said, "Probably buy a bunch of candy!" They laughed!

I said, "Nope! I am not going to buy anything!"

They said, "Nothing? Why?"

I said, "Because I'm going to save my money and buy a bike. If Jesus and I have a bike, we can get around faster and go a lot more places to explore together!"

Daryl said, "Oh, that's a good idea."

Dale said, "I don't know, I think you are going to want to buy some candy too! You know how you love candy!"

My dad walked in and said, "Hi, kids, what are you guys talking about?"

I went running up to Dad and jumped in his arms saying, "Guess what, Dad?!"

He picked me up and said, "What, honey?"

I said, "I am going to work hard, save my money, and buy a bike for Jesus and me!"

Dad clapped his hands and said, "My goodness! That is a wonderful idea! I love that idea, Linda!" Dad then said, "My oh my, Ma! It looks like these guys did such a good job that there is nothing else for us to do! Everything is working out so wonderful! I am proud of all of you and very thankful that we have such a good crew!"

He let my brothers know where the pinball machines and table and chairs should go. He also let them know where to put the booths. Dad asked me, "Linda, would you like to go to the post office with me?"

I said, "Sure, I would love to!"

Dad said, "We can just walk, it is very close."

This was the smallest town that I ever saw. Everything was close. When we arrived at the post office, there was an older man with grayish and white hair. He looked very smart. Dad and he started talking and I just listened and watched. The man talked to me too. He was nice. I liked him. Soon my dad said, "OK, let's go, Linda."

The post master said, "It was sure nice to meet you folks and look forward to having a restaurant in town! I can't wait to eat some good food for a change! You folks have a great day and don't work too hard!"

I waved bye to the nice man and he waved bye back to me. When we got back to the restaurant, everyone became busy. It seemed like I kept getting into everyone's way. I finally asked Dad if it would be OK if Jesus and I went for a walk. He said, "Sure, just check in so we know you are OK."

There was a grocery store close by. I went inside, and a lady started to talk to me. There was nobody else in there. She asked me what my name was. I told her, "Linda."

She said, "Oh, that is a beautiful name and did you know that your name means beautiful in Spanish?"

I said, "No, but my brothers and sister chose my name for me."

She said, "Well, your name means beautiful and you are very beautiful. Your name fits you perfectly!" She asked me, "What brought you to town?"

I let her know, "My parents are opening the restaurant down the street. They are very busy, so Jesus and I decided to get out of their way and go for a walk."

She asked me, "Would you like something from the store?"

I told her, "No, thanks, I haven't got paid yet. I must work more before I get paid."

She said, "Oh, you have a job?"

I said, "Yep, I am helping my mom and dad at the restaurant. My brothers work there too."

She said, "It is wonderful that you can all work as a family. I am excited for it to open! I know where I will be eating lunch."

I told her, "My mom is the best cook in the whole world! Everything Mom cooks is delicious!"

She laughed and said, "I can hardly wait. It will be so nice to have a restaurant in this town where we can enjoy some good food!" She asked, "Could I buy you a piece of candy and something to drink?"

I jumped up and down and said, "OK! I would love to have candy and something to drink! You are the best grocery store person in the world! Thank you!"

She said, "My pleasure! I am so glad you stopped in! You're welcome to come here and visit me anytime you like!"

I said, "OK, that sounds fantastic and the people in this town are so nice! I am already meeting friends!"

She said, "The candy is down this isle, you may choose whatever one you like, and the pop and drinks are back in the cooler."

She sure was nice! There was a lot of candy just like the candy store my brother Orville used to take me to. I picked out a sucker and an orange crush. I thanked her again and she said, "You are very welcome and it was a pleasure meeting you, Linda! Come see me again."

That was sure a nice lady. This town was so small that it didn't take long to get to the end of the block. I turned around and went back to the restaurant to check in. There was a lot of big trucks unloading stuff. Dad and Mom were busy dealing with lots of people. My brothers were busy putting stuff away for them.

Daryl asked me, "Where did you get the sucker and pop from?"

I said, "The nice lady at the grocery store bought them for me. She told me that I am beautiful and that my name means beautiful in Spanish."

He laughed and said, "Oh, OK, well you can go play and walk again."

Dale said, "Don't forget Jesus" and winked at me just like Dad used to.

Jesus and I decided to go explore the other direction. While we were walking, I had to go pee bad. We were close enough to my house that I could try and make it. I saw an older lady outside her home. She waved at me and said, "Hi." She asked me if I was OK. I told her that I had to pee badly. I was squirming and holding my private area trying to keep from peeing my pants.

She said, "Oh dear, come on in, you can surely use my bathroom."

I was relieved because I wasn't sure if I could make it to my house. After I used her bathroom, she said, "Do you have a minute to sit at the table with me for a bit?"

She wanted to know what my name was, so I told her. We went through the same exact conversation as the lady at the grocery store. She also let me know that my name means beautiful in Spanish. People sure were nice in this little town, I was meeting wonderful new friends.

After talking for a while and learning about each other, she fixed me a tuna fish sandwich. When we were eating, I made sure to give Jesus bites too. She asked, "What are you doing with your sandwich? It looks like you are sharing with someone."

I said, "My friend comes with me everywhere I go and I always share my food with him."

She said, "That is very nice of you to share your food. What is your friend's name?"

I said, "His name is Jesus and he is really nice! He likes everyone and he can be your friend too!"

She said, "Well, thank you, I would love to share your friend with you!"

I asked her, "Why do you pour water out of a jug instead of using your sink?"

She told me, "I don't have running water, so I have to haul it."

She also said, "I am almost out but didn't feel like getting any today."

I let her know, "We have lots of water at my house. If you would like, I could bring you some because I don't live far away."

She said, "That would be nice! Thank you for offering, that will really help me out." She gave me two jugs and said, "This will be all you will be able to carry at a time."

Jesus and I ran home as fast as we could and filled the jugs up. We couldn't run on the way back because they were too heavy. After giving her the full ones, she gave me two more empty ones. We did this over and over for quite a while and soon she had lots of water.

She gave me some juice and asked, "Would it be OK to give you a hug?" I let her and gave her a hug back. She said, "Your parents might be worried about you, so you better go let them know that you are OK. You and your friend Jesus can come visit me anytime you would like. I really enjoy your company."

I said, "We sure would, and I really enjoyed visiting with you too. Thank you for feeding us and visiting."

She said, "Thank you for getting water for me and sharing your friend Jesus with me. See you again."

We left and went to the restaurant. When we walked through the door, I was amazed at how wonderful everything looked. It was much better!

Everyone looked happy and said Hi to me. My dad said, "You must be hungry, Linda."

I told him, "No, I just ate."

He wanted to know where and what I ate. I told him, "First, the nice lady at the grocery store bought me a sucker and a soda pop. Later, I met another nice lady and she made me a tuna fish sandwich with some juice. She let Jesus and I eat lunch with her."

Dad said, "Wow! You have been busy! It sounds like you made some nice friends."

I said, "Yep! And that is not all, Dad. That lady has no water and has to haul all her water in jugs. I helped her do that."

He said, "That was sure nice of you to do that, I bet she appreciated your help."

I told him, "Everyone Jesus and I met today has been so nice! I sure love this little town!"

He smiled and said, "Well, there is so much to like about you, Linda."

I said, "Dad, guess what else?"

He smiled and said, "Come sit on my lap and tell me everything, Linda."

I jumped up on his lap, put my arms around his neck, and said, "All the ladies I met today told me that my name means beautiful in Spanish. They said it was perfect for me because I am beautiful."

He smiled and kissed my forehead and told me, "That's all true! You are the most beautiful girl in the whole world!"

I told him that I never knew that before.

He said, "Well, we learn something every day."

I told him to please tell Daryl and Dale that. He laughed and said he would be sure to do that. He asked me what I thought of the restaurant.

I said, "I absolutely love it! It sure looks nice!"

He said, "If you would like, I can teach you how to play the pinball machine."

I jumped off his lap and ran over to them. I was so excited! He did something with them and started showing me what to do. Soon, Daryl and Dale came over to us and asked Dad if they could play.

He said, "Sure, but you need to take turns and help Linda."

I tugged on Dad's shirt and whispered in his ear, "You need to tell them, Dad."

He asked, "What?"

I said, "About my name."

He said, "Oh! By the way, your sister's name means beautiful in Spanish, and now she knows that she is the most beautiful girl in the whole world so treat her like a princess."

Daryl rolled his eyes at me. Dad told him to be nice!

"This helps her confidence."

Daryl said, "OK."

I asked Dad what confidence meant.

He said, "It's your inside conscious."

I asked, "What is conscious?"

He said, "It's your brain's thoughts."

I said, "Oh, OK, I need some help with that."

He laughed and said, "Yes, we all do!"

I asked if I could play the game again. He told Daryl to let me have a turn. My brothers and I played for hours while Mom and Dad continued doing stuff. This was so fun! I could do this forever and ever! I told Daryl, "Wait, it's Jesus' turn."

Daryl said, "Jesus can't do this. You are just trying to get an extra turn!"

I started to cry and said I would help Jesus.

Daryl said, "OK, fine!"

We taught Jesus what to do and we all took turns and had so much fun! Soon, Dad asked us if we would like chicken strips and fries or cheeseburgers and fries. My brothers wanted cheeseburgers and I wanted chicken strips. It didn't take Mom long to make them. She cooked a lot faster here than at home.

Everything looked wonderful! Mom and Dad sat down and ate with us, after we prayed, of course. Suddenly, the front door opened and there were two men and two women. They were wondering if we were open.

My dad said, "Not officially. Tomorrow is our opening date, but I am sure we could fix you something."

He asked Mom, "What do you think, Mary?"

She said, "Sure, I am finished eating so it's no problem."

Soon the door opened again, and it was a man and a lady. They went and sat down at a table. My dad introduced himself and asked me if I would bring them water and menus. Dad was visiting with all the people when I brought the menus and water. This kept happening. People kept coming in and wanting food. Daryl and Dale helped Mom in the kitchen and Dad and Jesus and I were taking care of all the people. My dad went around to all the people and visited with them. He was having fun! I was busy being a waitress and milkshake mixer. This was fun! All of it! I loved my job! One man wanted to know my name.

I told him, "My name is Linda."

He said, "Oh! What a beautiful name!" He then said, "You sure are doing a good job! I think you're the best waitress I ever had."

I smiled and asked, "Would you like to know what I learned about my name today?"

He said, "Why certainly! I would love to!"

I said, "It means beautiful in Spanish."

He said, "Well, that fits you then, because you are beautiful."

His wife asked, "Do you know any Spanish?"

I said, "I learned how to count to 10 in Spanish when I watched Sesame Street."

She asked if I would do it for her, so I did. She smiled at me and said, "You are doing a good job, Linda, and we are sure glad that you are our waitress."

I said, "Thank you!"

Whenever the food was ready for a table, Mom would holler, "Order up, Table is ready."

That would help me out because all the tables were numbered so it made my job much easier. I would put the table number on the order, so Mom and I would both know. That was what Dad told me to do. I had lots to do and the people kept me busy. Dad and I both enjoyed talking to all the people. It was fun, and everyone was sure nice and friendly. I really felt like a big girl now. Dad took me to the till. He showed me how to find the prices and add it all up with the calculator.

He said, "You are doing fantastic and I am so proud of you! Everyone is happy and that is what we want!" I would take the dirty dishes to Daryl and Dale and they would wash them. Dad took care of the till and money. We all had important jobs. Everyone thought the food was delicious and thanked us. They all said they would come back! I kept finding money on the tables and bringing it to Dad. After everyone left and we got all the messes cleaned up, Dad had us all gather together.

He told us, "All of you did a great job and I am so proud of everyone! We make a good team and this was our first trial and it couldn't have gone better! I thank all of you! Mary, the people love your cooking!" He laughed and said, "And we weren't even open! If this is how business is going to be then we will stay busy! Most importantly the customers were happy. They will all come back! That's what we want! That is what will make this business successful and it took all of us to do just that!" He high fived us and said, "Now I shall give you your earnings."

We were all happy! I said, "Wow! That's lots of money, Dad!"

He laughed and said, "Yep! Not too shabby for the first day of work, huh?"

I asked if it was enough to buy a bike. He said, "No, you will have to work more and save more for a bike. Linda, just put it somewhere safe and keep saving."

Dad asked Dale and Daryl to help Mom clean up the kitchen and that he and I would clean the front. Dad brought me over to the till. Underneath the till he had a jar with a bunch of money. He said, "You know that money that people kept leaving on the table?"

I said, "Yes." He told me that those were tips.

"Tips is what they leave for the waitress for doing a good job."

He said, "Here you go! This is your money too." I was full of joy and all I could think about was getting a bike! Dad let me know that I had school in the morning.

He said, "First, you can come eat breakfast at the restaurant. Daryl and Dale will wake you because Mom and I must be here very early in the morning. After you have breakfast, I will bring you to school for your first day, OK!"

I said, "OK, Dad, do I get to always eat at the restaurant?"

He smiled and said, "I guess so."

This sure was a great day! I loved our new life! When I woke up in the morning, I was so excited to get ready and go eat at the restaurant! I got ready as fast as I could.

Dale told me, "You can go ahead and go to the restaurant."

When I got there, Dad gave me a great big hug, and introduced me to a lady that would be working for us and helping us with the restaurant when needed. She was very nice.

People were coming in and they were getting very busy. Dad asked, "What would you like to eat, Linda?"

I told him, "Toast with jelly."

He showed me how to make it and let me eat while he took care of the people. Soon Dad said, "OK, it's time to go."

Now I was getting scared to start a new school and Dad could tell. He asked me, "Do you have your rock?"

I said, "Oh no! I forgot it!"

He said, "It's OK, we can stop by the house and grab it and you can get one for your teacher too if you would like."

After we got the rocks, we went to the school. We stopped at the front desk and got situated. My teacher had black and gray hair. She had a mad-looking face and even seemed a little grumpy. I gave her the agate and she said, "Thank you." She showed me my desk and asked me to sit down.

I asked her if I could have another desk for my friend Jesus.

She looked at me strange and said, "Just sit down please."

I listened and felt very afraid to say anything. Dad talked to her for a little while and then came and talked to me.

He said, "Linda, Jesus can't have a desk in this room, but he can sit with you and share your desk, OK? Look, you're bigger now and you have a bigger desk. See there is plenty of room, sweetheart."

I said, "OK."

Soon, the other kids came and sat at the other desks. Dad gave me a hug and told me to come to the restaurant after school. When he left, all the kids were staring at me. I kept rubbing my rock. Two of the girls smiled at me and waved. I waved and smiled back. The teacher said we have a new student. She had me stand up and introduced me to everyone. She told me to go ahead and sit down in a very stern voice. I felt like this was the scariest teacher that I ever had. I didn't want to do anything to upset her. The rest of the kids did the same. I think we were all scared of her. She kept us very busy with a lot of work and we had lots to learn. It was hard work. The only fun we had was recess and lunch. Our class was very small. I think there were only nine of us total. At recess, I played with all the kids. The boys too! We all got along good. I was right, everyone was afraid of our teacher. Two of the girls wanted to play with me after school. I let them know that we could all walk to our restaurant and ask my dad. They said OK to that.

When school got out, we walked to the restaurant together. I introduced Dad to my new friends. I asked if I could play with them.

He said, "You all can play one game of pinball and then I will need you to work, Linda. Another day, you can play longer."

He got us some snacks and drinks. My new friends really liked my Dad. Soon it was time for them to go and for me to go to work. I thanked them and said goodbye. "I will see you in school tomorrow."

After they left, Dad asked me to go the post office and get the mail for him. When I got to the post office, the nice man remembered me and asked, "You here to pick up the mail?"

I said, "Yes, my dad asked me to." There was a lot, so he put it in a bag for me. I thanked him and let him know that I had to hurry because I had to get back to work.

He asked, "What is your job?"

I told him, "I am the waitress."

He said, "Oh good, I will stop in after work and have dinner. Make sure you're my waitress, OK."

I told him, "OK."

When I got back to the restaurant, Daryl and Dale were there. Everyone was busy, so I just said hi and gave Dad his mail.

Dad said, "Thank you, now could you wash your hands and start with table 8."

Most of the people wanted to talk to me and were very friendly.

I would let them know that I was going to be the best waitress in the whole world so that I could save my money and buy a bike. They thought that was wonderful.

Some would ask me, "What kind of bike are you going to get?"

I said, "One that would go fast so that Jesus and I could go everywhere together and get around fast."

They would look at me surprised and give me a great big smile. People sure were leaving lots of tips for me. I must have been doing a good job. Soon the door opened, and it was the post master. The restaurant wasn't busy anymore, so I got to visit with him a lot. We started talking about stamps and that he could help me start a stamp collection.

He told me, "I would love to work on starting you a stamp collection and when you come to pick up the mail again, I will have it ready for you."

I was so excited and thanked him. As the days moved forward, I stayed very busy. I was hauling water for the lady, collecting stamps, working, and going to school. I had plenty to do. My pillow on my bed had a zipper on the end of it. That was a good hiding spot for all my money that I was saving for my bike. My brothers would never think of looking there.

Soon the day came for Dad, Jesus, and I to go shopping for my bike. I had been waiting so long for this day!

Dad asked me, "Go get all your money and bring it to me, so we can count it up."

I got my pillow and brought it to Dad. I showed him the zipper.

He said, "That is a clever spot to put the money, but we will open a bank account for you to keep your money at the bank. That way it's always safe." I unzipped the zipper and to my surprise, a bunch of the money was gone.

There was only a little bit. I started sobbing and said, "Dad, Daryl and Dale found my hiding spot! I had so much money and now I hardly have any! I am so mad at them! This was supposed to be for my bike! I worked hard and saved for this! How could they do this to me?"

Dad grabbed me and hugged me. He said, "Linda, don't worry, honey. I will fix this. In the meantime, let's go get your bike! I will make Dale and Daryl pay you back. Remember I pay them. I can take what they owe you out of their wages."

I laughed and said, "That will teach them."

Dad said, "I was going to put your money in a savings account for you and Mom and I wanted to buy you the bike for working so hard and not being able to have hardly any playtime with your friends. We will still take what money you have left and put it in an account for you at the bank. From now on, you give me your money and I will take it to the bank, OK." That is what he did with his money and it worked great.

I said, "Thank you, Dad! You're the best dad in the whole world!" That was a good idea. I was still very mad at Dale and Daryl though.

He said, "OK, let's not let this wreck our day. Time to have fun! Let's go get you a bike!"

We went to town and stopped at the local gambles store. When we got to the bike section there weren't very many to choose from. I saw this black one with enough room on the seat for Jesus and me. It looked like it would go superfast!

I asked Dad, "Could I please get that one?"

He tried to pursue me to get the pink one with the white basket instead. That one was not fast enough, I could tell. I insisted on the black one. He finally gave in and let me have the black one. I was so happy! I couldn't wait to go riding with Jesus. Dad put the bike in the trunk and then took me to the bank with him. They were sure nice at the bank. They kept giving me things. I got a pen, paper, two suckers, gum, and even a balloon! This was the best day of my life! I loved this day! The best day ever!

Dad said, "OK, we better get going so you can ride your new bike!"

I said, "Thank you, Dad! You're my favorite person in the whole world! I have the best dad ever!"

He said, "You are my favorite too, Linda! You're the best daughter ever! I am so glad to see you so happy!"

I said, "Oh, I am happy and love this day!"

When we got home, Dad had me sit on the bike. He told me to be careful with the bar between my legs.

He said, "This is a boy's bike, that is why the bar is there."

I said, "I don't mind, I like it anyway."

Dad adjusted the seat and made it more comfortable for me. He said, "Go ahead and ride it. Make sure to check in at the restaurant like you usually do and have fun!"

I said, "Thanks, Dad, I will!"

He said, "Take the day off and enjoy your new bike! I will be having a talk with your brothers."

Jesus and I went biking all over! I was right, the bike really did go fast! We visited the lady and filled her jugs for her. We visited the postmaster. He helped me get my stamp collection started. He gave me a green photo album to put the stamps in. As he was giving me the stamps to put in the album, he also explained what they meant. He sure was smart! I learned a lot of good things about these stamps. He told me that these stamps would be worth a lot of money someday. He even gave me The Boston Tea Party! That was my favorite and his too! They were so beautiful! I loved my stamp collection! This really was the best day of my life! It just couldn't get any better! I thanked the postmaster for doing all of this for me.

He said, "I enjoy it. I will continue giving you more stamps to add to the collection."

I was super excited! Jesus and I were so happy! Here is a picture of the post office taken in 2018. It is still there but many years later.

Chapter 7

My Dad

After time passed and I was getting older, I began babysitting to make money too. Many would have thought I was too young to be babysitting. I felt the same way but did it anyway. My parents became friends with many people so that's why I started babysitting. Their friends knew people that needed someone. I was still working at the restaurant too, so I was very busy working a lot. Now I was in 6th grade so I was going to be going to a different school in a different town about 6 miles away. It was the same school that Dale and Daryl went to. I would ride the bus. The bigger kids and teachers referred to me as Dale and Daryl's little sister instead of calling me by my name. My teacher was much nicer than my previous teacher. This was also a much bigger school and there were more kids in my class. My teacher's name was Mr. Johnson. Everyone in the class seemed to really like him. All the kids in the class were very nice to me. I became closer to some more than others. My dad seemed to be very tired and sick a lot. He was doing a lot of doctoring. I was so worried about him. One day we had to drive about 80 miles so that Dad could have a surgery. They found a lump on his lung that needed removed. I felt so scared for him.

Before he went into surgery, I gave him a big hug and kiss. When the medical staff took him, I started to cry. My brother Daryl put his arm around me and comforted me. Mom had tears too. Dale was comforting her. After a while, they let us see him. He looked puffy and different.

He was acting very strange. I never saw my dad act like this before. He was really being silly. I was so happy that he was alive. I kept holding his hand and kissing it. His eyes closed with a smile on his face and he went to sleep.

Mom said, "Let's let Dad rest and go get something to eat."

Before walking out of the room, I asked Mom if I could just have a quick second. I brought Jesus over to Dad and said, "Don't worry, Dad, I am giving you Jesus to borrow. He will take good care of you and stay with you until you're all better."

Dad opened his eyes and said, "Thank you, sweetheart. I love you so much, Linda."

I told him that I loved him so much too. He closed his eyes and I left with my mom and brothers. I knew that Dad would be OK, and that Jesus would take good care of him. We went to the cafeteria in the hospital and ate. It felt strange not having Dad with us. Everyone was quiet and seemed so sad. I let them all know that I borrowed Jesus to Dad and he would be with him until he is all better. I said, "Don't worry, I know Jesus very well and he will take perfect care of him."

My mom said, "Thank you, Linda, that is so sweet of you."

I said, "Don't worry, Mom, Jesus will fix everything!"

My brother Daryl put his arm around me and said, "Linda, you are very special and that was nice of you to think of Dad!"

Dale agreed! We all seemed to be getting closer to each other. Even though this was a hard time for all of us, some good was happening too. Soon we were done eating and headed back to go see Dad.

When we got there, Dad was sitting up watching TV and seemed to be doing better. The doctor was there and talked to us about all that was going on with Dad and how his surgery went. What they took out was cancer and he left one nodule that he wasn't concerned about at this time. He let us know that Dad would have to take it easy for a while. The doctor said, "He will be able to go back to work as soon as he recovers. He should feel a lot better soon."

We were all so thankful! I got up on the bed and cuddled with him. I said, "I told you Jesus would fix everything, Dad."

He smiled, rubbed my head, and said, "Thank you for sharing him with me. He sure is helping me."

I said, "Yep! You can keep him until you're all better!"

He held me tight and gave me a big kiss. His eyes were watering. I had never seen my dad cry before.

I said, "Dad, it's OK, please don't cry."

He said, "These are happy tears. I am so happy to have all of you."

I sighed with relief. I loved my dad with all my heart. I didn't ever want him to be sad. He was my Hero. We brought Dad home and let him rest. I went for a bike ride. It was kind of scary without Jesus. I knew Dad needed him right now, so I would just have to be brave.

I checked on the lady with no water and she said, "I am good, but you can stop back in a couple days." She then asked, "Are you OK, Linda?"

I said, "This is my first day without Jesus. My dad is very sick, so I borrowed Jesus to him until he is better. It feels different without him and I don't like how this feels. It feels way better having Jesus!"

She said, "You sure have a good spirit."

I asked her what that was, and she said, "A spirit is what God created in you and the rest of us."

I said, "You have a good spirit too and I really like it."

She said, "Do not worry, Linda, everything will be OK," gave me a big hug that made me feel better.

I went to the post office to see my friend there. He was so happy to see me and had a bunch more stamps to give me.

He asked, "How is your dad doing?"

I said, "He is resting."

He said, "You sure love your dad, don't you?"

I said, "Yep! He is my favorite!"

He smiled and said, "I can tell. You are very lucky to have that relationship with your dad. Don't worry, Linda, everything will be OK."

I said, "Oh, I know, Jesus is taking care of him!"

He said, "I love how you love Jesus! I can tell that you always have Jesus with you, that's for sure."

I said, "Yep, he is my best friend in the whole world!"

As time went on, Dad was getting sicker and even having seizures. We were spending a lot of time at the hospital and sometimes would have to call the ambulance. He was diagnosed with small cell lung cancer and was just getting sicker and sicker as the days went on. We had to close the restaurant and move to a different town. We moved to the same town my school was, so I could walk to school instead of riding the bus.

Here is a picture of our house that we moved to. These pictures are taken many years later in 2018 but these places are still there. The house still looks the same as it did when my family and I lived in it.

Here is a picture of the Tastee Freeze across the street from our house. This picture is also taken in 2018 and to my surprise, it is still there.

We ended up getting Dad a hospital bed. My dad was always hurting and hardly able to even eat. I felt so bad for him, I didn't know what to do to help him. All I could do was cuddle, rub his hand, and be there.

We had some friends that lived outside of town and would sometimes go play at their house. They had an older son who really loved playing with kids.

He would spend more time playing with the kids than hanging out with the adults. He was very funny and would take turns giving us piggyback rides. We would come out here quite a few times so we got to know Ben really well. He would dress up in a woman's clothing sometimes and let us fix his hair. He had long hair for a man. He always wore a cowboy hat.

One time I was upstairs in the bedroom with Ben fixing his hair while he was dressed up as a woman. As I was curling his hair with the curling iron, he had his dress pulled up and his private area showing. I could see everything. I was in shock and felt my heart racing with fear. Jesus whispered to me to go tell someone and to not be alone with him. I walked into the other bedroom and told his brother that Ben had his you know what out.

He laughed at me and I said, "I am serious, he really does! Please come with me because I don't want to be alone with him."

He said, "OK."

All the adults seemed to think it was great that Ben enjoyed playing with the children and would make comments that he fit right in with the kids. Even though he was an adult man, he was very silly. When his brother came back to the bedroom with me, Ben hurried and pulled his dress back to normal as he was sitting waiting for me to finish his hair.

He said, "You know I am running out of time. I need to get to town so we can play this again another time."

I was relieved and his brother Paul and I went downstairs.

I said, "Paul, thank you, that was so scary."

He said, "You're welcome."

Paul and I didn't talk about it again. At that time everything was in the moment so I never would think about the next day until that day was here. A few days later my mom and dad were at the hospital. I walked home from school and nobody was home. Suddenly, Ben was there. I didn't even hear the door open or hear anyone knock. He startled me. I talked to him for a while and then asked him if he wanted a cookie. He ate some cookies with me.

He asked, "Can I use the bathroom?"

I said, "Sure."

While he went to the bathroom, Jesus whispered to me to take his hand and leave with him fast. I didn't understand why but listened to him because Jesus knows everything. We lived across the street from a Tastee Freeze. Jesus had me go in there with him. I didn't have any money, but I had Jesus!

There was a game room in back with a PacMan machine. Jesus and I sat back there together. Soon, Daryl was tapping me on the shoulder.

He said, "Why are you over here by yourself instead of being at home?"

I said, "Because Jesus made me come here."

Daryl said, "Well, I guess that worked out since nobody was home. Well, come on, we need to get home, OK."

I said, "Is Ben still there?"

Daryl said, "No, nobody is home yet. Why was Ben at our house?"

I said, "I don't know, he was there when I got home. When he was using the bathroom, Jesus made me come here."

He said, "I'm glad because Ben is weird. Something is not right about him. I don't understand why he was even at our house. That is weird too."

After a few days had passed, I was upstairs sleeping in my bedroom. My bedroom had a bathroom with no door on it and it was just a toilet. My brother Daryl slept in the room beside mine. I could see his bedroom door from my room. He would always leave his door open in case I would get scared. While I was sleeping, I had a nightmare about a spider. I woke up screaming like crazy! Daryl came running in and asked, "Are you OK, Linda?"

I said, "Yes, I just had a bad dream. I was dreaming about a spider."

He said, "No, I heard someone come in here."

We saw Ben's cowboy hat and it looked like he was kneeling, trying to hide in my bathroom. Daryl put his finger to his mouth motioning me to be quiet. He grabbed my hand and took me downstairs. Daryl woke up Dad and told him what was going on. Even though Dad was very weak, he went upstairs. When he came back down, he said nobody was up there.

Daryl said, "Dad, we saw him. He was hiding in Linda's bathroom. He was here the other day when you and Mom were at the hospital too. I found Linda at the Tastee Freeze. She said Jesus made her go there."

Dad was very upset! He was on the phone with the police officer that I would babysit for sometimes. After this, I never saw Ben again. We found out later that he also did this with other children in town. Dad wanted me to sleep with him from now on. I liked sleeping with Dad. It was comforting, and I felt safe. Dad would moan in his sleep and move a lot. I felt so bad for him because I knew he was hurting so much. I had a talk with Jesus. I thanked him for always helping me and being there for me. *My Dad really needs you so bad. Please help him, Jesus. Please take his pain away.* Jesus didn't respond.

I said, "Jesus, can you hear me?"

Jesus said, "Yes, your dad is being soothed by you and me, that is all the help we can give him right now."

When Jesus would talk to me, it wasn't like how we talk to each other using our mouth and words, it was done through our head. I could still hear him in my head but nobody else could. He would just put in my head what he was saying and I could understand him. I just had to be quiet and listen. I was so thankful that I could at least sleep by my dad and cuddle with him. I really hated him being so sick and hurting so much.

As time went by, my dad was too sick to live at home with us. We had to put him in a nursing home about 20 miles away from where we lived. My older brothers Kevin and Orville, and my sister Elaine and her new baby Chynna came and stayed with us. Chynna was so cute! Dad got to hold her and sure loved that. I was missing a lot of school because we were spending a lot of time at the nursing home with Dad. I would go visit with all the old people and then climb in bed with Dad and cuddle.

One day my dad wasn't opening his eyes or talking. My mom said that he was in a coma. She felt that he could still hear us though. It was weird. It was like he went for a long sleep and wasn't waking up. He was like this for quite a long time. One day, I was lying next to him and my mom was sitting in a chair by his bed. He woke up! He sat up in bed and said to us, "I had the most amazing experience! It was so beautiful that I can't wait to go back. Linda, now I understand about the rainbow colors and how beautiful everything is!"

I asked Dad where he was. He said, "I was with Jesus and all the angels." He looked at mom and said to call Pastor Thorp right away. "We need to get Linda baptized. We need to get this done as quick as possible!"

My mom looked confused. I was confused too. Dad went from sleeping for days to being wide-awake and full of energy. He had a lot of stuff to say and do. It was amazing! I was so happy for him. I asked Dad if Jesus talked to him about me. Dad said, "Boy! Did he ever! Jesus really loves you, Linda, but he wants you to be baptized."

I asked, "What's that?"

"It's a special ceremony with Jesus that Pastor Thorp will do, and that way Jesus can live inside you. It needs to be done and we should have done this a long time ago."

They got on the phone with Pastor Thorp and arranged for it the next day. It would be after school. I was so excited! My Aunt Phyllis, my mom's sister, would be there with me.

She was also going to be my godmother. My parents also had a special event planned at the nursing home. It was going to be their 25th anniversary party. They planned it for April 11th so that it wouldn't take away from my 12th birthday party. They had been planning this for quite some time. My dad told my mom that we needed to change the date to the 8th instead of the 11th.

He said, "We must! Don't worry, Linda, we will celebrate your birthday too."

This would be on the correct day, so I thought that was a good plan. We usually always celebrated their anniversary and my birthday together, being as my birthday was on their anniversary, it just worked that way. My mother was not pleased with this.

My mom said, "Hilmer, can't we just leave it? That would mean that I will have to call all these people and inform them."

He said, "Don't worry, Mary. The kids and I will help you do this. Orville and Kevin can probably take care of it."

She looked disappointed but said, "OK then."

Dad also wanted to talk about some financial things with her. He had lots to say. I was so happy that he was so full of energy and life. Mom seemed to be overwhelmed though. I hadn't seen my dad like this for a very long time. He was smiling and so happy. He also seemed like he was glowing. Dad gave my mom lots to do and think about. Dad had a way to get others to listen to him and do what he wanted. After a lot of talking, Dad asked me to come up on the bed and cuddle with him.

He said, "Linda, you are my favorite girl in the whole world!"

I told him that he was my most favorite Dad in the whole world too. I said, "Please tell me more about your time with Jesus, Dad."

He said it was the happiest he ever felt or dreamed he could feel. It was so peaceful and beautiful and everyone was so happy and full of joy! I smiled and said, "That's how I feel with Jesus too! Isn't he something!"

He said, "He sure is! Too bad the rest of the world doesn't understand this! It would sure help if they did."

I asked if he got to play with Jesus. He said, "No, we didn't play but we talked a lot and did a lot of other things. I understand Linda why you always want to play with Jesus!"

I said, "He is the best! He is different than my human friends. Jesus understands everything all the time. We never get into fights or arguments because he is always nice. He loves everyone in the whole world. He told me that. Dad, I wish you could be there for my baptism."

He said he wished he could be too, but Aunt Phyllis would be there with me. "You will be fine."

Soon, it was time for us to go. Mom and I said our goodbyes to Dad. My brothers, sister, her baby, and husband were at our house waiting for us when we got home. I hung out for a while, and then went and played with Jesus. I let Jesus know how happy I was that he fixed my dad and that he was with him. I told him that all of us thought he was in a coma but instead he was with you and now he was all better.

I knew you would fix everything. I also am going to get baptized and my birthday will be celebrated with Mom and Dad like it usually is. Everything is much better! Thank you, Jesus, My best friend ever!

During this time, I had been missing some school. Mr. Johnson was very helpful with that. I still had homework and assignments to do while I was missing school. He didn't want me to get behind. He also let my classmates know about Dad, so they knew why I was gone so much. Soon it was time to go home, eat, bathe, and go to bed. My mom let me know that I would go to school the next day. After school, I was to come straight home.

She said, "Pastor Thorp and Aunt Phyllis will be here waiting for you. Everyone else would be with Dad. After it is over, Aunt Phyllis will bring you to the nursing home. It probably won't take that long."

I loved my Aunt Phyllis a lot. She was very nice. I was happy that she would be with me to help me. I said good night to everyone and went to bed.

Chapter 8

Jesus Lives in Me Now

The next day at school, it was kind of fun to see everyone again. Everyone was actually very nice and acted like they really did miss me. Especially my friend, Melinda. She always acted more grown up than the other kids. I think that's what I loved about her so much. She had the biggest heart, just like Jesus. I had a great day! I really wanted to be with Dad, but it turned out fine. The school bell rang, and it was time to go home! I ran as fast as I could all the way home! When I got home, Pastor Thorp and Aunt Phyllis were at the dining room table, visiting. I gave Aunt Phyllis a hug and Pastor Thorp gave me a hug. He smiled and asked if I was ready.

I said, "Yep, I sure am! I can't wait for Jesus to live inside me!"

He laughed and said, "OK then, let's get started! I am going to explain a few things to you, so you understand what we are doing, OK?"

After explaining and reading about baptism in the bible together, I learned a lot. It even says in the bible that God wants everyone to be baptized. I wonder if that is what's wrong with some of the people. Maybe they just need to get baptized so Jesus can live inside them. Maybe they don't know about it.

The room was a little dark with a dim light. We began the ceremony. During the baptism, the room became very light and pleasant. It was glowing. When Pastor Thorp finished, I suddenly felt different. I felt like how my dad described how he felt while away with Jesus. Things seemed so clear and everything seemed so beautiful. I never noticed all the colors like this before. They were so pretty. I loved everything and everyone so much! It felt so good! Everyone in the whole world should get baptized because it would make them feel so much better. That was an experience I will remember for the rest of my life! Pastor Thorp had my aunt sign some papers. He gave her everything to give to my parents. I even got to keep the candles! They were blessed and special candles. I was so full of joy, I couldn't stop smiling! My Aunt Phyllis and I left to go see my dad.

Pastor Thorp went back to the church to do some stuff. While on the way to the nursing home, I talked my Aunt Phyllis's ear off. She just kept smiling at me and letting me talk. I loved her so much! She was so nice and very pretty too. I suddenly realized what beautiful eyes she had. They were a bluish green and sparkled. When we got to the nursing home, I got out of the car and went running to Dad.

Aunt Phyllis said, "I will meet you in there."

I went bursting into my dad's room and jumped up on the bed with him. I got a big hug and started telling him everything! My brothers told me that I needed to be gentle with Dad because he was hurting.

Dad said, "You are OK, sweetie, tell me more."

I had so much to share with him that I talked his ear off. He kept smiling at me and let me talk away!

My Aunt Phyllis and Mom stepped out of the room to go take care of some things with the changes of the party. My brothers, sister, her baby, and husband decided to go get something to eat. Dad and I cuddled, talked, and laughed. We had so much fun. This was the best day of my life! Nothing could be better than this day! I loved every single second of it! I was so happy and so was my dad. I just wished everyone could be as happy as us! A lot of people just seemed so blank. After a while, it was time to say goodnight and goodbye to Dad. Everyone was tired. Normally, I would be sad leaving Dad all by himself, but this time I wasn't. I didn't need to be. Jesus lived in me now. I had clear eyes like a brand-new pair of glasses. I saw everything much better. Dad gave me a big hug and kiss and said goodnight. I still felt like talking a lot for some reason, I even felt so much smarter. I talked all the way home non-stop.

Mom said, "Well, that drive sure went fast! I am so glad you're feeling so good, Linda!"

I said, "Mom, you sure are beautiful. Your eyes are so pretty and sparkly, just like Aunt Phyllis'."

Mom said, "Oh, thank you. You are so beautiful too."

After getting in the house, it was time for my bath. It was truly fascinating to me how everything had a colorful rainbow effect. My bubbles in the bathtub even had it! This was the best bath I had ever taken! I loved seeing through my new eyes!

Chapter 9

Mom and Dad's Big Day

Today was going to be a very special day! It was my 12th birthday party and Mom and Dad's 25th anniversary party. I was so happy that my dad had Mom change the date from the 11th of April to the 8th. I knew Jesus had good reason behind this. We should all celebrate on the real date anyways because you can't change the date you were born or married. I was hoping to go downstairs and see all my presents. When I got downstairs, everyone looked stressed and were rushing around.

I said "Good Morning" to my mom, hoping she would say happy birthday and give me a present.

She said, "Hurry up and eat, Linda, we have lots to do today."

I was kind of sad; I knew if my dad were here, he would have woken me up with a present. He would always do that and sing happy birthday to me. I figured maybe the rest of the family would do something for me, so I went over by them. They told me that I needed to stay out of the way instead. Maybe everyone was tricking me and had a surprise for me. When we arrived at the nursing home, I jumped out of the car and went running in to see Dad. Of course, I jumped up on his bed like always. He gave me the biggest hug and sang happy birthday to me. He said, "You are 12 today. Look how you have grown up into a beautiful young girl. I am so proud of you, Linda, and love you so much my sweet, Linda! You're my favorite!"

I said, "You're my favorite too, Dad, and I sure love you too!"

He started to cry. I asked him if they were happy tears. He said, "Yes, I am so happy, and this is such a special day!"

I asked, "Dad, do you have a present for me?"

He said, "No, Mom is taking care of that. I'm sure you will get presents later today."

I said, "Oh good! Dad, this is a great day!"

He said, "It sure is! We will see many relatives and friends that we haven't seen for a while. Mom is going to play her accordion too! We will have all kinds of fun today."

I asked Dad, "Did Jesus give you new eyes to see with?"

He wanted to know what I meant. I said, "Yesterday at my baptism, Jesus gave me new eyes and a new heart." I told him about all the new things I was seeing and how different I felt.

He said, "Yes, I understand, I guess Jesus did do that for me."

I said, "Isn't it much better?"

He said, "Yes, much better, honey!"

We cuddled and watched TV for a bit. Soon the others came to Dad's room. When Daryl walked in, he laughed and said, "I guess we don't have to worry about where Linda is, do we?" I wasn't sure what he meant by this, but the others thought that it was funny too. Mom gave Dad a hug and kiss and let him know that they needed to go get the room ready for the party. Dad told her, "Go right ahead, Linda will keep me company."

After everyone left the room, Dad and I had each other all to ourselves. We talked, cuddled, laughed, watched TV, and had so much fun together. I absolutely loved spending time alone with Dad. Soon the nurses and Mom came into the room to get Dad and me. It was time to go to our party! The nurses had to help my dad get into a wheelchair. This was very difficult for them to do. Dad was so weak and hurting so much that he was sure having a difficult time doing this. It was hard to watch my dad hurt like this. I felt so bad for him and wished I could do something to take his pain away and make him strong again. I couldn't help but to silently cry. Every pain he felt, I felt as well. I asked Jesus if he could please take him to this place called Heaven. *My Dad enjoyed being with you so much, Jesus, and he is just hurting too much. It is hard on our whole family watching him suffer like this. At this point, you're the only help we have.*

I made a deal with Jesus. *If I give you my dad and let you take him to Heaven, will you please let me be with him again someday? I love him so much that I would rather let you have him and take good care of him then watch him live this miserably. That's a lot of love that I carry in my heart!*

Suddenly, I got a bunch of odd shivers all over my body. They felt kind of like goose bumps. They were different though. They were comforting and like Jesus was affirming that he was listening to me and was present.

Dad looked at me and said, "I'm OK, Linda. Please don't worry, honey. We have a party to go to, don't we?"

He smiled and winked at me. I wondered how he knew. Could Dad read my mind? He asked to hold my hand while Mom pushed him in the wheelchair.

When we arrived, people stood up and started to clap. There were a lot of people and a lot of food. It was noisy with all the people. The place was decorated beautifully. They also had balloons all over that matched the decorations. I took notice of a big beautiful cake. I asked if it would be OK if I went and looked at the cake. By the cake were a bunch of presents as well. That of course struck my interest too.

Dad said, "Sure, but please don't lick the frosting because we need to take pictures."

I laughed and said, "OK."

My dad sure knew me well! When I got to the cake, to my surprise it said Happy 25th Anniversary Mary and Hilmer. I wondered if maybe I had a separate birthday cake somewhere. I looked all over but couldn't find my cake anywhere. I then went to see my presents. Strangely, all the presents were also for Mom and Dad. There wasn't even one with my name on it. I decided to go ask Dad where my stuff was. He was very busy with lots of people surrounding him. I squeezed my way through and said, "Dad? I have something I need to talk to you about."

He said, "Linda, it's not very nice to interrupt people when they are talking. Whatever it is, you will need to wait your turn."

I told him that I was sorry and walked away. I found a spot where I could sit and wait for Dad to be less busy with people. I could keep a good eye on him. As I watched Dad with my new eyes, I realized how very handsome he was.

He looked so happy. This made me smile and made me happy too. People sure loved my dad. I guess it was my day to share him. Soon it was time to eat. We said a prayer, blessed the food, and everyone got in line. I figured this would be a good time for me to finally be able to visit with Dad. I started walking towards him. Before I got to him, Mom started to wheel him to the cake.

People were taking pictures of them. I decided I might as well sit down and eat. I kept my eye on Dad the whole time, just waiting for that free moment. He just kept getting piled with people. Sometimes he would smile and wave at me though. This party started to feel like it would go on forever. Finally, people started to leave. After Mom and Dad said goodbye to everyone, Mom started pushing Dad back to his room.

Dad said, "Stop. Where is Linda?"

I said, "I'm right behind you, Dad."

He said, "Linda, please come hold my hand and walk by me. Please tell me what you wanted to talk to me about earlier, honey. I didn't forget about you, I just got overwhelmed with people. I was keeping my eye on you though. Thank you for being so good."

As I was about to talk to him, two nurses came and grabbed the wheelchair from Mom. I had to let go of Dad's hand as they brought him into the room. When we arrived at Dad's room, they started to continue hurting him like last time. This time Dad was hurting so much that they decided to give him a pill and wait for it to take effect before continuing. I was thankful that they were going to help him because nobody should have to go through such torture and pain. My eyes were watering. Every pain Dad felt, I could feel with him. I wished I could take away his pain so badly. I prayed and told Jesus, *please don't let him hurt like this anymore. Please, Jesus, take my dad and bring him to Heaven with you and I beg of you with all my heart. Please.* Those shivers that I talked about earlier arrived again.

My dad looked at me and said, "Linda, it's OK, honey. I'm OK. Don't worry, honey."

Wow! My dad really could read my mind!

The nurses decided to try and put Dad into his bed. My dad was suddenly acting very goofy. He was slurring his words and everything he was saying wasn't making any sense at all. The nurses were laughing and said, "Yep! The pill is working."

I couldn't understand why he was acting so different because of a pill. I decided right then and there that I never wanted to take a pill. I had never ever seen my dad act like this. They got him in bed and changed his IVs, took his blood pressure, and some other things. The nurses told my mom that he would be sleeping for the rest of the night. Mom said, "That's good, he had a very big day today."

Mom looked over at me and said, "I am very tired too."

I went up to Dad and gave him a kiss on his forehead like he usually did for me. We left and headed for home. On the way home, Mom said, "Did you have a fun time, Linda?"

I told her there were too many people, but I had fun watching her and Dad have fun.

She laughed and said, "Yes, there definitely were a lot of people that showed up. A lot of people sure love your father."

I said, "Yep, they love you too, Mom. Thank you for making this party so special for Dad. I know you put a lot of work into making it perfect. You did a fantastic job, Mom."

She said, "Thank you, Linda."

When we arrived at home, I figured it must be my turn. I would imagine that my cake and presents were waiting for me inside. I knew my brothers and sister were all inside. I bet they would say surprise and give me everything I had been dreaming of. I was so excited to see what they have done for my birthday! When I got into the house, they were at the dining room table. I looked at all of them and smiled and waited for a second. They were busy talking.

I looked around the house trying to find a cake or presents. I just wasn't finding anything. I walked up towards Mom, she said, "Linda, you need to get to bed. It was a very big day today."

I said, "OK" and gave her a hug and said goodnight to everyone. My sister, being deaf, bent down to me and asked if I was OK. I realized how beautiful she was. She had long shiny brown hair. Her eyes were the shape of almonds and big and brown. She had my dad's perfect nose and a big wide smile with perfect white teeth. Her skin was this perfect olive color like Dad's. She was petite with a perfect figure. She looked like a Barbie doll. I was so busy looking at her that I forgot what she had asked me.

She asked again, "Linda, are you OK?"

She talked funny because of being deaf. I smiled at her and nodded my head yes. Even though she talked funny and other people had a hard time understanding her, I never did. Sometimes when she would babysit me, she would teach

94

me different things in sign language to make it easier for us to talk to each other. She grabbed me and hugged me. She said that she was proud of how good I had been and told me that she loved me. We said good night to each other. I did what everyone wanted me to do and went to bed. Before falling asleep, I got watery eyes again. I was thinking about how I didn't even get a birthday. I was feeling so sad about it. I guess it got skipped. I felt as though someone was hugging me and got those shivers again. Even though I couldn't see anyone, I felt someone.

It sure felt good and comforting. I suddenly realized that my birthday got given to Mom and Dad this year. I guess that was OK, we could skip my 12th birthday and let my parents have it. It felt like my dad kissing my forehead but bigger. Those shivery goose bumps came back again.

Whatever or whoever it was, I sure liked how it felt. It felt so soothing. Everything felt OK. I felt safe, content, and happy again. This was good! Then I dozed off and fell asleep.

Waking up the next morning was the normal routine for a couple of days. I got ready, went to school, and then to see Dad after school. This time when we arrived to see Dad, he had a lot more stuff hooked up to him than the previous day. He even had tubes in his nose. There was a lot of beeping noises. I couldn't jump up on the bed like I usually would. Dad just kept sleeping. He hardly spoke at all. The nurses told my mom that they were just keeping him comfortable. I just sat and prayed to Jesus to please just take him to Heaven. He wasn't living anymore. He was just sleeping. *Jesus, I think they are giving him too many pills and now he isn't acting alive anymore. Jesus, please just take him and take care of him. He deserves to be happy. He has always been such a wonderful human being to everyone. He deserves to be happy forever and ever. I know that with you, Jesus, he will be.*

My dad woke up and said, "Linda, it's OK. I am OK, honey."

I suddenly got those shivers again. I walked up to him and grabbed his hand and held it. I said, "Dad, how do you read my mind?"

He said, "Honey, I love you so much! Don't worry, my love. I don't want you to be sad. Everything will be OK, Linda. God's got this! Trust God, OK?"

I said, "OK, Dad."

I kept holding his hand and rubbing it and kissing it. Sometimes he would squeeze my hand. Even with all the tubes and stuff, I couldn't help but to stare at what a beautiful man my dad was. I couldn't imagine loving anyone like I loved him. He was the best of the best! God gave me the best Dad, I just know he did.

My mother wanted to go home. I didn't want to. I wanted to stay the night with Dad.

Mom said, "We have to go home, Linda."

I argued with Mom and said, "Please, Mom! Please! Dad needs us to comfort him and love him. Mom, please? He really needs us, I just know he does. Can't we just stay with him tonight?"

Mom said, "Linda, please, don't make this so hard. I will let you skip school tomorrow and you can spend the whole day here, OK?"

I agreed, gave Dad a kiss on the forehead, and he smiled and squeezed my hand. Mom and I had a quiet ride home. I still felt so bad leaving Dad and couldn't understand why I couldn't just stay with him. I learned to just listen to your parents, even though sometimes it was hard. This was one of those times. If I was older, I would have stayed right by his side. I wanted Mom to turn the car around and go back. I begged her.

She said, "Linda, don't worry, you will see your father in the morning. I am exhausted and need to get my rest too. Maybe you should think of my feelings too."

I said, "Mom, I am sorry for arguing with you."

She said, "It's OK. All our emotions are running high right now. You just love your father so much! Linda, I understand, I love him too. I get it. I wish I could just stay with him too. It's hard to leave him."

I said, "It sure is, Mom. I hate leaving him alone with those nurses just in case they try to hurt him. I guess he isn't alone though. He has Jesus, Mom. He told me not to worry, that God's got this."

Mom said, "Yes, God has this one! We will be OK."

I said, "I love you, Mom."

She said, "I love you too, Linda!"

When we arrived at home, we went to bed right away. Before I went to sleep, I asked Jesus if he could be with Dad and take good care of him for me. I let Jesus know how badly I wanted to spend the night with him but couldn't. *Jesus, I love how you take such good care of me. I love you so much for it, but could you please just do me a big favor and go be with Dad for me. I will be OK, I would rather you be there. He needs you.* I got those goofy shivers and fuzzy feeling again. After that, I calmed down and went to sleep.

Chapter 10

Saying Goodbye to My Hero

The next morning, I woke up to Mom shaking me and telling me, "Hurry up, we got to get to Dad right now! The nursing home called and said we need to come now!" I got dressed as fast as I could and ran downstairs as fast as I could. I hurried and got in the car. Daryl, Mom, and I took off. This is the fastest I ever saw my mom drive. When we arrived, I went running as fast as I could.

Daryl said, "Linda, wait!"

I didn't listen. I had to hurry and get to Dad. When I ran into Dad's room, Oh no! Dad's eyes were weird looking, and half opened. His mouth was open. He wasn't breathing. He looked empty like he wasn't there anymore. I grabbed his hand and said, "Dad? Dad? Please, Dad? Dad? Oh no!" I started crying so hard it felt like my dad squeezed my hand. It was a definite squeeze.

My mom and Daryl said, "Linda, come here."

I told them, "No, he squeezed my hand. Hurry, get some help, hurry."

Mom was sobbing, and Daryl grabbed me and hugged me and said, "He is gone, Linda."

A nurse came in and shut Dad's eyes and his mouth. Pastor Thorp came in and we all circled around Dad while we prayed. I kept holding Dad's hand, but I wasn't getting any more squeezes. He was empty. I guess he was in God's hands now and with Jesus. He was gone. I felt like crying but decided to help my mom out.

She wasn't doing too good. I gave my dad a kiss on his forehead and I got them shivers again. I swear Dad smiled. He always did when I kissed his forehead. Maybe he came back to get one last kiss from me. I went up to Mom and told her, "Mom, Dad smiled."

She cried and said, "Come on, Linda. We need to go now."

I grabbed her hand and said, "Mom, even though Dad is empty right now, you should go say bye to him. Maybe he will smile for you, Mom." She listened to me.

She hugged him, brushed his hair off his forehead with her fingers and came over to me and said, "Thank you, Linda, that was a good idea. I even feel better."

I told her, "Don't worry, Mom, I will help you with whatever you need. We will be OK. I promise I will take good care of you, Mom."

She said, "How did I get such a sweet girl?"

I said, "Well, we can do this! At least Dad isn't hurting bad, taking pills, or sleeping all the time anymore. He wasn't even living. Now he is having fun with Jesus in a very special place! He has a new home now and he will be there waiting for us! Mom, Dad told me that everyone is happy in Heaven! Isn't it nice knowing that he is happy now?"

She said, "Yes, but I still am going to miss him."

I felt her pain. We both started to cry. I then felt bad and guilty that I prayed for this to happen. Everyone around me was hurting and crying so much! *Oh no! What have I done? I didn't mean to make everyone feel so sad.* Everyone around me was hurting and crying so much, but I asked Jesus to help all of them. *Did I do a bad thing, Jesus?* The shivers arrived again, and a rainbow appeared out of nowhere. I felt better and knew that Dad was with Jesus in a good place! I decided I would just be nice to everyone and help them. My dad told me that not everyone has the eyes that God let us have. I sure wish they did, because that would fix everything. Dad always knew what he was talking about. I trusted Dad with all my heart and soul. I am going to miss his smiley face, hugs, cuddles, kisses, and all our talks and time we spent together. I was not going to miss my dad suffer so much though. I loved him so much that I couldn't bear watching him live that way. That wasn't living.

We had company at our house. All my brothers and sister came and stayed with us again. People kept bringing us food. My family wasn't hungry for all this food, but I sure was. I prayed so much for my family to just feel like me. I prayed that they would be thankful for all the wonderful times we had with him. We were so lucky to have the best Dad in the world. He was the best husband for Mom. I never saw my dad yell, be angry, or mean. He was always so happy and such a joy to be around. Dad was so full of love. He had a special gift with animals and loved all animals. He lost all this when he got sick with cancer. His life completely changed in one day and so did ours. The nicest thing about all of this was, you see, Jesus was with all of us; even if the others didn't know it, I sure did! My family, relatives, and friends started sharing fun stories with my dad. It was fun to hear all these stories. It was so nice to see everyone laughing! I knew my dad would love this! He would never want any of us to ever be sad. *This is good. Thank you, Jesus, for answering my prayers. Now everyone will be all right. Thank you! I love you so much!* Soon we were planning his funeral. It had to be done!

Being as Dad had been in the army, they would be doing something special for that. It was going to be a big funeral. Dad was liked by many. Pastor Thorp helped all of us so much through this time. Mr. Johnson, my teacher, let my classmates know why I had been missing so much school. Some of my friends came to see if I was OK. That meant a lot. I loved all my friends. Loved my whole class. We were like our own little family. We all got along great! That evening when it was bedtime, I thanked Jesus for giving everyone smiles instead of tears. I prayed for Dad's funeral to go well. Because he sure did deserve it. *Thank you, Jesus, and I love you so much!* I fell asleep feeling warm and fuzzy. As I was sleeping, I felt Dad tapping my shoulder. I could even smell him! These shivers were a little different than my usual. Soon I saw my dad's face and he said, "Linda? Can you do me a big favor?"

I asked, "What do you need me to do, Dad?"

He said, "They are going to fold my flag wrong tomorrow. I know that you don't understand any of this and I do not expect you to. I just ask that you please let your brothers and Mom know this for me, OK? Tell them to make sure the flag is folded right, OK? Thank you, my sweets I love you so much and I am doing wonderful." I asked if he was with Jesus. He said "Yes" and smiled and waved. He then just disappeared, and the smell left and so did the shivers. I felt at peace and fell back asleep. When I got up the next morning, I wondered what Dad was talking about with the flag. I didn't understand, but knew that I needed to give this message from my dad. *He is counting on me and I don't want to let him down.* I ran downstairs and everyone was at the dining room table visiting and some of them were eating.

I said, "Mom, Dad came to see me last night and this is what he said." I told them exactly what he said.

One of my brothers said, "Linda, you have quite the imagination."

I got upset and said, "No! It's not my imagination! Dad woke me up! I smelled him."

Mom stopped me and said, "It's OK, Linda. Everything will be OK."

My brother Orville said, "Wait a minute. Linda knows nothing about a flag. She is too young to understand or know any of this. I don't think this is her imagination." He gave me a hug and said, "I believe you, Linda. Thank you for giving the message and I assure you that I will personally make sure the flag is folded correctly. Dad's last wish, right?" He then winked at me. "Linda, you know what Dad's last words to me were?"

I said, "What, Orville?"

He said, "Dad told me to take care of Linda. He said that girl is so full of Jesus and love! I wish I could see what she ends up being because I know it will be wonderful, whatever it may be! She is one of a kind! Treat her like a fine piece of china! I trust you, Orville." I got watery eyes and realized Dad loved me as much as I loved him. I thanked Orville for telling me this. We hugged, and Orville said, "Don't worry, I will keep my promise to Dad."

We all had to dress up for Dad's funeral. Mom said, "By dressing up is how we show respect for God and Dad." Everyone looked amazing. My mother looked stunning! We went to the church. We met with Pastor Thorpe and each took turns seeing Dad in his casket. We all had watery eyes coming out of the room. Orville wanted to know if I wanted him to come with me. I said, "No, that's OK, I'm fine." When I got up to Dad, he looked very peaceful but empty. He wasn't there anymore. I thanked him for all the wonderful times we had together. I thanked him for loving me so much! I also thanked him for being the best dad ever! I told him to have fun with Jesus forever in Heaven! Those shivers came upon me. I had his hand, but it was so very cold. I kissed his forehead and it was cold too. He just wasn't there. That was OK though because I knew where he was. Yes, I would miss him every day of my life, but he was in the best place ever. It was much better than here. I just knew that I would see him again and when I will, it would be a forever thing. That made me happy to just know this. When I came out of the room, Orville was waiting for me. I looked at him and said, "Dad is fine. He is happy with Jesus." He took my hand like Dad used to and we went and joined the rest of the family.

Pastor Thorp instructed us to be seated up front in the reserved seating area. Orville stayed by me and kept holding my hand. As we were walking to our seats, everyone was staring at us and there were a lot of people. I got nervous and reached for my agate that Dad gave me. Oh no, I realized that I had a dress on and forgot my agate at home. I was really in a panic. Orville grabbed my hand tight and squeezed it.

He whispered, "It's OK, Linda. I am here and will help you." I wondered if Dad gave him the ability to read my mind. I figured he must have! I smiled at Orville and felt better. I was thankful for him to be taking such good care of me. I knew Dad picked the right one to oversee me. Pastor Thorp did a wonderful service for Dad. The music was so beautiful. People had so many different stories that were fun to hear. The men dressed up in army outfits were putting on quite a show. This was all so amazing! They even shot their guns off in the air. After all this excitement, the pall barriers were folding a flag. Some of them had apparently been drinking alcohol.

That wasn't good of them to do on this special day. I nudged Orville and asked, "Is this what Dad was talking about with the flag?" The flag was folded in red and white stripes in a triangle shape. Orville nodded yes to me. They handed it to my mother. She looked at Orville with a shocked look on her face. I asked Orville, "Is it folded wrong?"

He said, "Yes, don't worry, I will make sure it gets fixed."

I sighed with relief and said, "See, Dad was right." Dad was always right just like Jesus. Jesus was always right too. When we gathered together as a family, Orville grabbed the flag from Mom and said, "Out of respect for Dad, we will fix this now." He asked my other brothers to help him.

They all looked at me with shocks on their faces. Daryl said, "I guess Linda was right."

I said, "No, Dad was." They figured out how to fold it. It was blue with white stars now. It looked much better and beautiful. That must have been important to my dad for some reason. Everything ended well, Thanks to my brothers. Dad would be happy and proud of them. After my dad's burial, it was late enough that we went home and spent time as a family. We were all relieved that this was over but all of us had an empty spot in our hearts. It was just not the same without Dad's presence. He added so much to our family and to our home. Knowing that we had each other, we were all thankful for that. We grew closer through all of this and helped each other through each day as it came upon us. Even if the sun was shining, it felt as though we were all in the dark.

Dad always brought joy to our home setting and loved to see us smile. It was different now and we would just have to accept it for what it is. The only way we could gain joy in our home again was to be truly thankful for the time we got with him and to live each with doing the best we could with God. We needed to trust God, and everything would be OK. He would be missed while we were on this earth but in the end, we shall be together again.

And I took notice to Mom drinking and going out with her friends a lot. As time went on, my mom got some money from some land that Dad had. All my siblings got a certain percentage of this. I didn't get any because Mom was still taking care of me. I was just too young. This made me feel bad, but I understood. Mom took her friends and me on a fun trip to Oregon. She also bought a new home for us. It was an old house that needed lots of work. Orville was very good at doing everything that the house needed to be remodeled. After he finished doing everything, the house looked beautiful. Mom picked out the colors and carpet in the bedrooms and living room. She had orange kitchen counter tops with beautiful oak cabinets.

Mom got a new stove, fridge, double oven which she always dreamed of and a new microwave oven. We put a fireplace in the living room and got all new furniture. Everything looked so nice. They did a fantastic job. They also worked well together, and Daryl helped too. I pretty much stayed out of the way and played with my friends. It was so nice having Orville around. I really didn't want him to leave. Although Daryl and I got close with each other, we were all we had. We didn't have anyone else. Mom decided to date again. Daryl and I weren't excited about this at all. Soon she began dating a man named Tom. He was Ben's father. He was also one of the pall bearers that messed up my dad's flag at his funeral. He had been a friend of Mom and Dad's for quite a few years. Mom assured me that Ben would never be allowed in our home or in my presence. She also assured me that Tom was nothing like his son Ben and he was upset with Ben for doing the things he had done. She said, "Tom is a very nice man and I enjoy being with him. Remember he is a friend of Dad's, so he would never do anything to hurt us or harm us in any way." She explained that Tom had been a friend or her and Dad's for years. That made me feel better. Daryl and I started to realize that Mom was smiling a lot more and seemed so happy. She was humming and singing again. She also was playing the organ and the accordion again. That was nice to see. That was the most important for her to be happy. I was pretty sure that my dad would want her to be happy. We already knew that nobody could ever replace our dad. He was the best. Daryl and I would never be able to call anyone else dad. We couldn't do that. It wouldn't feel right. Mom would go dancing and go out a lot with Tom. Daryl and I were spending a lot more time with each other. He was a senior and I was in 7th grade. He was a football star and had a beautiful girlfriend named Cheryl. She looked like Princess Diana.

She was super nice too. I was happy for him. Soon it was Jesus and I spending time together. Sometimes I would spend time with my friends as well. I had this one friend named Melinda Bischoff. I considered her my best friend. I loved her whole family. They were all wonderful people.

Melinda's mom, named Pat, would let us use her kitchen to make cupcakes for the boys football and basketball team. We were cheerleaders, so we decided to do something nice for the guys. It was a lot of fun. Melinda was very caring and nurturing. She helped me get through some tough times. She was also there for me when my dad died. She would always have a very special place in my heart and I will always be grateful for our friendship. God blessed me with such a beautiful person to have as a friend.

I would also do some babysitting for my mom's friend Bonnie. She turned into being a very close friend of mine as well. She was the most beautiful human being. I just treasured the time I spent with her. She was so full of Jesus and didn't even know it. She was my mom's friend Vicky's younger sister. Vicky was like an aunt to me. She was always making me smile. I could talk to Vicky about anything. She was very good at giving advice. Bonnie also had a twin sister named Becky. Becky was very special too.

I immediately liked Becky when I met her. She was very loving and kind. I was honored and blessed to have these wonderful people in my life. My life was going great. I had a lot of wonderful friends. Daryl was a fantastic guy and I really felt close and connected to him. Mom stayed busy going out with her friends and Tom. Daryl stayed busy with football and being with Cheryl. I stayed busy with school, sports, cheerleading, and hanging out with friends.

Chapter 11
Satan Tried but I Denied

I had a full day and was feeling very tired. I decided to go home and take a nap. When I got to our house, nobody was there. I went to my bedroom and lay down. It didn't take me long to fall asleep. Suddenly I felt a tap on my shoulder and woke up. I looked, and nobody was there.

I still was very sleepy, so I shrugged it off and fell back asleep. Again, I awakened by the same tapping. This time I suddenly had these cold chills, nothing like the chills Jesus gives me. These chills felt scary and bad, so I immediately ran to my door and locked it. I became so afraid and didn't know why. As I was standing by the door, I heard footsteps coming towards it. They were long paced footsteps. My heart started beating so fast I could hear it thumping. The footsteps stopped at my bedroom door. All I could do was stare at the door handle and try to stay quiet. That was hard to do, my heartbeat was making so much noise. As the door handle jiggled, I hurried to my bedroom window and went out of it. I saw Tom's pickup in the driveway and ran as fast as I could. It was hard to run because I was barefoot. I told myself to just keep running and did, even though it hurt to do it. So many things were running through my mind. I didn't even know where I was going, I just knew that I had to keep running.

It came to me that Jesus was the one tapping me, and I thanked him for doing that for me. "I am so thankful! Thank you, Jesus."

Daryl suddenly drove up in his orange and black Nova, all decked out. He pulled over and asked me if I was OK. I didn't have any proof of anything, so I told him yes, I was fine.

He said, "Get in, we can go for a drive."

When I got in the car, he asked me where my shoes were. I didn't know what to say to that, so I just said, "I had a blonde moment."

He knew me too well and said, "You aren't that blonde, why aren't you wearing shoes?"

I said, "I had a bad dream while napping and was scared so I got out of our house without thinking, so yes, it was a scared blonde moment." Then he wanted to know what my dream was about? *My goodness how much is this guy going to put me through?* I felt like I was on the stand and I truly didn't want to lie so I needed to shut him up.

I said, "Daryl, I am fine, let's cruise to our spot and jam out to 'Down Under.'" He had a very nice stereo system. Daryl always had nice things and was very fussy with his stuff too.

He smiled at me and said, "OK, but just so you know, you can talk to me about anything, Linda. I am always hear for you." He then put the song on and turned it up very loud. We sang at the top of our lungs. He drove very careful and slowly. We always would drive out to the cemetery and park the car and play music and sing to the dead. We didn't know anyone in the cemetery, so we just figured that we would entertain them all. If they could hear us, I believe we made their day! We would laugh, and Daryl would do these goofy voices.

I was in the 7th grade and Daryl was a senior in high school. I had not been touched by a boy or even wanted to. I think I had a crush on one boy and that was when I was in first grade. I really didn't feel attracted to any of the guys in my class because we were like family. I noticed some of them were better looking than the others but that was it. I spent more time with my friends and had much better things to do than have a boyfriend. I was so busy with bike riding, swimming, visiting, and hanging out with all my friends. I also would babysit a lot. I had so much to explore and learn. I was learning the truth about Tom. Maybe he was like his son Ben. He sure was trying everything in the book to touch parts of my body that have never been touched by anyone. I didn't tell anyone because I knew my mom was so happy and didn't want her to feel bad.

Daryl worried too much about me, so I did not want to stress him out. I was trying to think what had I done to cause this? I couldn't think of anything but felt I had to have done something to cause this. I didn't realize it at the time, but that was something Satan does. When a person is feeling down, he attacks because they are weak. He loves to toy with people when they are unprepared and feeling weak. Even though Daryl and I were having fun, this just kept my mind busy.

Daryl finally said, "We better head home because I'm getting hungry."

I said, "OK."

When we arrived at home, Tom's pickup was still in the driveway. I felt OK since Daryl was with me. When we got into the house, Tom was sitting at the table drinking his Vodka like usual. Daryl went to the fridge to get something to eat. As I was walking by him, Tom grabbed my butt. I jumped and yelped.

Daryl looked at me and asked, "What is wrong?" I looked at Tom and said, "A big ugly spider was there, but I will stomp him." I usually didn't like conflict, but I looked at Tom straight into the eyes and glared at him. He made me mad! He had no right to grab my butt! *He is my mom's boyfriend. What do I do? Mom's working at the noodle plant about 20 miles away. I can't tell her. She is so happy. I would ruin everything!*

My body was like a stick. My friends had boobs but mine weren't showing up yet. I couldn't understand what I was doing to make this happen. I started to change. I was choosing different clothing to cover up my body more. Keeping this to myself, I started to get very depressed. I lost my energy and happiness. I began distancing myself from my friends and spending a lot of time alone. My grades were falling, and I started missing school. The principle of the school was our neighbor. His name was Mr. Hoffman. I adored him so much. He tried talking to me and was very worried and concerned about me. I just told him that I wasn't feeling good.

He said, "If I can help with anything, let me know."

I felt like he could read through me. I just said, "OK." As time went on, Tom kept sneaking grabs. Even though he did it often enough that I should have been used to it, it would still startle me. When I would go to bed, I would lock my door, put a butter knife between the door and the paneling and move my dresser in front of the door. This became my nightly routine. All I knew was that I needed to keep this ugly spider out of my room. I lived in fear and walked around on eggshells. I hated how I felt. Daryl kept asking me if I was OK and I would just tell him that I was fine. When Tom was at our house, he was always drinking a lot of vodka. When he would use the restroom, I would dump out a lot of his vodka and add water to his bottle. He wouldn't even notice. One day I felt like getting out of the house. Somehow through this time I had lost my best friend Jesus. I felt so bad about myself that I honestly believed in my mind that Jesus probably felt the same about me. Again, I didn't know at the time that this is exactly how Satan works. I felt guilty and ashamed for so long that I felt Jesus might be upset with me and disappointed. I was yearning to have him back. I missed his friendship and love so badly. I had a pond behind my house that nobody could see. I went to it. I decided to go there and ice skate which was one of my most favorite things to do. I had made up a routine from the theme of ice castles song. It was my dad's and my favorite song. My dad had watched me ice skate many times to this. He would tell me that someday I would be in the Olympics' and all self-taught. I hadn't ice skated since my dad had died, but felt the urge to. When I put my skates on and started to play the jukebox, all my fears went away. I finally felt at peace. It had been a long time since I felt this way. It felt so good! I asked Jesus to please forgive me for whatever I had done to make such bad things happen to me.

Please be my best friend again. I miss you so much and really want you to please give me another chance. I truly miss you with all my heart and soul and love you so much. Please, Jesus, come back to me! Please help me get out of the situation I am in and help keep me safe.

Suddenly, the sun was shining so brightly, and I had them good shivers again. I felt warm and fuzzy again. It had been a long time that I felt this way. I knew Jesus was back and there with me.

Oh, what a relief! I smiled up at the sky and said, "Thank you so much! I love you so much!" I wished that I could have my mom back. She spent all her time with work and Tom, I hardly ever saw her anymore. She hadn't spent any time with me for a long time. My principle seemed more concerned about me than her. As I wished this a very strong smell of roses lingered in the air. It was beautiful but strange because it was winter. In North Dakota, our winters are very cold, and roses do not grow in the winter. I kept looking around to see why this smell was here but there was nobody. I decided to pretend my mom was watching me and spending time with me. I did my routine over and over. I had a beautiful song, beautiful routine, precious sunshine, and the most beautiful scent of roses surrounding me! Jesus was back, and this day was very good! I was so happy and felt so good. I felt like my mother was watching me.

Everything was perfect! I just did my routine over and over and enjoyed this moment like there was no tomorrow. I decided that I should head up to the house knowing that Daryl was home by now and probably wondering where I was. I thanked Jesus for this special day. I looked up at the sky and said, "Dad, this was for you. I love you and miss you so much, Dad!"

When I got back to the house, I saw Tom's pickup. "Darn it! Here goes my great day!" I asked Jesus to please keep me safe. I went inside. As usual, Tom was sitting at the kitchen table with his vodka bottle and his dog. I asked him where Daryl was. He said that he went to the store to get a few things. That made me feel so much better. I hadn't taken my ice-skates off yet because I was so thirsty and needed a glass of water.

I was reaching for a glass and Tom got upset with me because I still had my ice skates on and said that I shouldn't wear them in the house. I was thinking I would just check in and go skate again. He said, "Take them off before you wreck the floor." He sounded very angry, so I apologized and said that I would take them off. He came up behind me and said, "That is not all you are going to take off." He grabbed me and started to undo my pants. I asked him to please stop. He told me to just shut up and not say another word. His dog started barking. My eyes where watering and I was so frightened I didn't know what to do. He told his dog to shut up and started getting very aggressive with me. He pulled down my pants and underwear as he pulled down his own pants. I started crying and sobbing. His dog started barking again. Suddenly Daryl walked in. *Oh, thank goodness.*

Daryl freaked out and shoved him and said, "Get away from her and leave her alone! Don't you ever touch her again!"

Tom pulled his pants up and said, "I thought you were going to your girlfriend's house."

Daryl said, "I did but she wasn't home. What do you think you're doing to my sister?"

As I pulled up my pants and underwear, Tom and Daryl were ready to fist fight. I got in the middle and asked them to please stop. Tom told us to get out of the house and we were never allowed back. Daryl said, "Come on, Linda." I still had my skates on but went with Daryl. I was so embarrassed and ashamed. I felt so awful. The truth was out now, and I had no control over it. My heart was racing, and I couldn't stop crying.

Daryl said, "We aren't finished yet, Tom! Linda, hurry up and get in the car."

My coat was still in the house, so I was so cold and shivering. Daryl cranked up the heat in the car and gave me his coat to put on as we drove off.

We parked at the cemetery. He gave me a big hug and said, "I am so sorry. I should have known by the way you had been acting that something was going on."

I hadn't had a hug from anyone since Dad died and this hug felt so good, I wouldn't let go.

I told him, "I'm so glad you came home when you did."

He asked, "Did Tom hurt you?"

I said, "No, you came just in time."

He asked, "Has Tom ever done this before?"

I told him, "No, nothing this bad."

He said, "But he has done stuff to you?"

I said yes. Daryl wanted to know what? I told him everything. "Sneaking grabs, trying to get into my room." I told him that I would even pour his vodka out and add water. Daryl wanted to know why I didn't say anything. I told him that I was afraid to.

He said, "Linda, you have to always talk to me. I promise I will always protect you."

I sighed and asked him if I was going to be in trouble. He said, "Of course not, you haven't done anything wrong. Tom is messed up in the head. He has done something wrong but it sure wasn't your fault." Daryl decided that he needed to call Orville and let him know what was going on. We went over to his friend Darrin's house to use the phone. I stayed in the car being as I didn't have any shoes. Even though this beautiful day had turned so awful, it felt good to talk to Daryl and not have any secrets anymore. I was thankful that Daryl was taking over. Daryl came to the car and told me, "Orville wants to talk to you."

I asked, "How? I have my skates on."

Daryl said, "Just take them off when you get inside." We went inside the house and I took off my skates. When I got on the phone with Orville, he sounded angry. He said, "This is what we are going to do, I will call Mom and deal with her. I am going to get you a train ticket to come out here to Oregon. We need to get you out of there until we can get Tom away from Mom and all of you, OK?" This sounded good to me because this was no way to be living.

I said, "OK."

He said, "I will get the soonest ticket I can for you, OK?"

I thanked him, and he told me, "Try not to worry, everything is going to be OK. Listen to Daryl. He will keep you safe until you get here, OK?" Orville's voice softened, and he said, "Linda, you didn't do anything wrong. You didn't deserve this. We are going to help you, OK?"

I said, "OK, thank you, Orville."

He said, "I love you, Linda."

I said, "I love you, too."

He said, "I suppose I better talk to Daryl again."

I said, "OK, thanks again and here is Daryl." I gave the phone to Daryl.

After Daryl got off the phone with Orville, he said, "Just stay for a moment while I go and talk to Darrin and his parents." Daryl and Darrin were best friends, so Darrin always felt like a brother to me. He was adopted by his parents. He was the only Indian in our little community. Everyone really liked Darrin a lot. He was always very respectful and had a great sense of humor as well.

When Daryl came back to get me, he said, "We can stay here until we can get this fixed. I talked to Darrin's parents and they offered for us to stay here. They also offered for me to live with them after you leave, since I will be graduating this year anyway. I think that's maybe a good idea. That way I don't have to put up with Tom. Hopefully Mom will get out of this relationship soon."

Darrin's parents were so kind and loving. I felt very safe. Well, my life sure changed in a hurry! The next morning my mom and her friend Vicky came to get me. Vicky was a close friend of ours. She was like family. I thought of her like family. I adored her, and she was so fun to be around, yet if I ever needed any advice, she was good at it. I trusted her. She was always happy, and I can still hear her laugh to this day. She had a son named Sam that I would babysit. I enjoyed him so much. He never misbehaved and was easy to take care of. He was the sweetest boy. When Mom and Vicky picked me up, they had my suitcase packed and clothes and shoes for me.

Mom said, "Go get ready, we are going to drive to Minot and you will take a train from there to Oregon. Your oldest brother Kevin and his girlfriend Nancy will pick you up from the train station. You will stay with them until Orville gets things figured out."

I said, "OK." I loved my brother Kevin and I had met his girlfriend Nancy and really liked her too. Nothing at all was mentioned about Tom. They acted like everything was normal, so I didn't say anything neither. When we arrived at the train station, the train was already there. We had to hurry and get my ticket and check in. After we did that, we had to say goodbye as I got on the train. It was sad for me to say goodbye to my mom. I wished so bad that we could have spent more time together. Now I didn't know what was going to happen or when I would see her or Daryl again. They helped me get in the train and waved goodbye. I started to cry so hard and couldn't stop. I had never experienced these emotions before. Didn't my mom love me? She was just letting me go. How could she do this? As I looked out the window at them while the train was leaving, I cried even harder. I wished none of this had happened. I felt as though Tom had ruined everything. I also felt as though Mom was choosing Tom over Daryl and I. So many disturbing thoughts were going through my head and I just kept crying.

My heart felt like it hurt. I understood what people mean when they say your heart is broken. My heart really felt broken. Not only did I lose my dad but now I had just lost my mom and my brother too. How come this was happening? I tried to stop crying but it wasn't working. I had never cried like this before. All I wanted was a mother.

Suddenly that same smell of roses surrounded me. That was the same smell from when I was ice skating. I stood up and looked around the train. There was an old couple close to me and they waved at me and smiled. They looked like a nice Grampa and Gramma. I waved back. This smell was weird because it was the middle of winter. There was snow on the ground. Where was this smell coming from? It sure smelled good though and for some reason it comforted me, and I felt soothed. Like a baby must feel in its mother's arms. I was still busy minded though and my thoughts were not good.

The more I thought my mom, Tom, Daryl, not saying goodbye to any of my friends, the more I cried. I just could not stop crying. I think I could flood the train if it kept up. The old couple kept bringing me Kleenex and making sure I was OK. They were so kind and loving but I didn't want to tell them why I was crying. That night on the train, I couldn't sleep. I think I cried myself sick. I was feeling horrible. I couldn't stop coughing.

I would be hot and sweaty but was shivering and cold. My hair was wet from sweat. My cough was getting worse as the night went on. I would smother myself in the pillow; I had to try and cough less noisily so others might get some sleep. Finally, the old guy gave me a pill to take and said, "This will help you with your coughing."

I took it and said, "Thank you."

I think that no matter how quiet I was trying to be, I was still keeping the whole train awake. I felt exhausted and weak. My head and body were sweating but I was so cold. I kept wiping the sweat off me with some of the Kleenex. Pretty soon the older woman came and put a blanket over me. She gave me a pillow and some water. She said, "You're very sick, sweetie. You poor thing." I just listened to her sweet voice and took in her comfort. She was so nice. I was too weak to talk, I just wanted to sleep so bad. Between coughing and crying, I really was ready for sleep. It never happened. I still coughed all night long and that pill didn't help. The elderly couple were giving me cough drops, but I would still cough while trying to suck on them. One time it almost went down my throat. That scared me. I didn't need to add choking to the list. The couple kept an eye on me all night and kept taking care of me. I never felt this weak and tired before. I kept sweating and shivering. The lady would put a cool washcloth on my head and freshen up my pillow and blanket. She would give me sips of water too. I felt as if I wasn't getting any breaks. I was thankful for this couple helping me. They were like angels sent to me. Finally, we arrived in Portland, Oregon. The old couple carried my luggage and stayed with me until my brother Kevin and his girlfriend Nancy found me. The elderly couple let Kevin and Nancy know how sick I was and that they should get me to a doctor right away. They also informed them that I was running a bad fever as well. Kevin and Nancy thanked them and said they would. We got in their vehicle and drove to Salem. I was still coughing, and my chest hurt so bad. It was difficult to breath. They brought me to the hospital. The doctor said, "You have walking pneumonia." He looked at Kevin and Nancy and said, "It's a good thing you brought her in. She is very sick." He let them know what to do with me and gave me medicines to take. He said, "She will need to rest and stay hydrated. She will not be able to start school until she gets better. If she gets worse or doesn't get better then bring her back in right away." We got everything I needed and then left the hospital. When we arrived at Kevin and Nancy's house, they showed me my room. All I wanted to do was sleep. I went right to bed and honestly think I fell asleep before my head hit the pillow. There were a lot of siren noises that I wasn't used to hearing before. I was so tired that I didn't even care. I just wasn't used to all these sirens and new noises coming from a small town. The city had a lot of noise. I fell back to sleep again and throughout the night I would wake up to the sounds but would doze back to sleep again. Normally these sounds would have made me scared but I didn't have the energy to worry about it.

Chapter 12

My New Life

I think that I slept for two days other than taking medicines and drinking fluids. When I woke up, I had several thoughts going through my mind. I realized that I was starting over. I left my nice little cozy town and was now in a city. I would be starting a new school. I was worried about my mom with Tom. I lost trust with people. I trusted myself and Jesus but that was it. I was in a scenery change and atmosphere. I had to pull myself together and be strong. It was time to put the armor on and go for it! I was going to prove to myself and others that not only could I do this, but I would do a great job at it too! Nobody was going to hurt me again! I just needed to be brave and strong! I could and would do this! I had a resentful feeling towards my mother but still loved her very much! I just wished so badly that she was with me. I started to cry again even though I was trying to talk my mind into being tough. That smell of roses suddenly appeared again, and I stopped crying and felt at peace. Whatever this smell of roses was must really be strong because I could smell it clearly and my nose was all plugged up. I felt comforted, loved, and peaceful. It was like how my mom would make me feel when she loved me, but better. It was soothing and soon I fell back asleep. I woke up to Kevin and Nancy checking on me. I could hear them, but my eyes were so heavy, I didn't open them. I heard Nancy say, "It smells good in here."

Kevin said, "Yeah, it does, it smells good like roses." They covered me up better and Kevin said, "We need to let her rest." I heard them leave the room. It felt like I was sleeping with roses everywhere. I was on my fourth day of recovering and sleeping more than I had ever slept before. As I began this day, I put it in my mind that I was going to conquer the world. I was not going to let any negativity trouble me and I would just cling to Jesus! Everything was going to be fine!

I just need to put my armor on and go for it! When things began to settle down and I was totally recovered, I moved in to the basement of this lovely Catholic family, the Hetterscheids. They had a daughter named Chris that I had met when I was riding my bike. We immediately became friends and got along great! Mom and Orville arranged for me to live there and go to school there. I think they had 13 children, but Chris was the only one left in their huge house. Chris had a bedroom upstairs but spent most of her time with me in the basement or riding our bikes together. We would walk a lot too. The school I was going to was amazing. It was a smaller town close to Salem and my brother Orville lived close by. He would always come get me and do stuff with me when he could. We would go on drives, and he would take me in the mountains. He loved being in nature just as much as I did. We found some great swimming holes together and he knew all the spots that nobody knew. He worked for the State of Oregon and his wife was a Social Worker for Marion County. They made good money and were so happy.

It was pleasant to be around them. Orville and I would camp and do lots of fun stuff together. He would let me bring my friends with me on some of our adventures. I feared nothing! I was on top of the world! I could go to the top of the mountains on some of the most dangerous roads and wasn't even a tiny bit scared! I would jump off the highest cliff without thinking anything of it! I never had a fear of heights mainly because I think I spent a lot of time on my brothers' shoulders growing up, so I was always higher than most. I loved life! Oregon was so beautiful compared to North Dakota. I loved the mountains and the crystal-clear water. I couldn't imagine living anywhere else when we could live with all this beauty! God is amazing to have created all of this! I looked forward to meeting him some day, imagining what he must be like. I know he sure had a fabulous son! I knew him well and that made me love God so much! To be able to create all these marvelous things for us to enjoy! He must be something! He thought of everything and didn't leave nothing out! One of my most favorite spots was the Oregon Coast. Lincoln City and Newport were only an hour away. The sound of the ocean was so peaceful. It made me feel so comfortable just like it was home. I would walk the beach with Jesus many times. We would see all kinds of neat things every time we did this. I could walk and run forever without getting tired. I especially loved running! I felt so free when I would run! My brain would go into a different mode of happiness! I could run and run forever! I loved running!

At school Chris and I became good friends with a gal name Theresa and another one named Kim. Theresa had been with a lot of guys and was even very sexual. Chris, Kim, and I had not been with any guys and were still virgins. We would ask Theresa a lot of questions about sex out of curiosity. All of us became so close. We trusted each other with our lives! We knew that we would always be there for one another no matter what. That was nice to have this security. Kim and I tried out for dance team together. Chris was into tennis and Theresa was not into any school activities. She was just interested in having fun and guys! I knew Kim would make the dance team, but I wasn't sure about myself. Kim was extremely flexible and could do the splits without any problem. I had to practice, and Kim would push down on me. One day I got it because of all her help. I could do the splits and touch the floor with no struggle. Now maybe I could make the dance team because that was one of the requirements. If we made dance team then somebody in school would pin a rose to us and that was how we knew we made it. Kim got a rose pinned on her right of way. She was so happy, and I was so happy for her! I knew she would make it, but she didn't think she would. She had very little self-confidence, so I worked on that with her. I thought she was stunning! She had beautiful brown hair. Her eyes were a unique color of gold and light brown. They had the perfect shape and always looked like they were smiling even if she wasn't. Like my dad's eyes except his were brown. Everything on her face was flawless. She had the most beautiful skin. She wasn't only beautiful, Kim was extremely intelligent too. Her personality reminded me of Daryl. Daryl was extremely smart too. They could get

A's without even studying. It was like their brains were sponges that absorbed everything and didn't miss a thing! Chris, Theresa, and I didn't have the sponge brain. We had to study! Kim had a huge insecurity about her weight. She thought she was fat. It was starting to annoy me because this bothered her so much. I decided to help her. We would exercise together, and she would eat less. I loved exercise and it felt like the right thing to do with her, so she could feel better about herself. I kept thinking that I must not have made the dance team because there were a lot of people with roses but not me. Kim and I were talking, and she said if I didn't make it then she would not accept. I told her that wouldn't be right, but she didn't want to do it alone. She needed me. This made me feel bad because I didn't want her to lose this opportunity over me. I prayed for her to please help her with joining the dance team and help her to feel comfortable to take this opportunity. As soon as I got done praying a gal came and pinned a rose to my shirt. Kim and I were jumping up and down with excitement. My prayer instantly got answered. *Thank you, God, you amaze me!* We had practiced every day with the dance team. I had been used to being a cheerleader, but this was very different. Our dance team instructor was very tough. She wasn't a bit friendly and just very powerful even though she was short. She was a woman full of determination and was going to shape us up into being what she expected.

We worked hard to try and please her. Nobody on the team was given any slack. It felt like being in the army. I was getting burned out with this because it was too negative for me and dramatic. I already had told my mind not to let people disrespect who I was and to stay away from negativity. There must be something out there that would be better than this. I talked to Kim about quitting the team. She begged me not to. I let her know that this really wasn't my cup of tea. I loved dancing, but I wasn't happy at all. The dance instructor made us pile on makeup, pull our hair back, and put on fake smiles. She was rude and hardheaded. There was no compromising and would make me feel bad instead of good. Nothing positive ever came out of her mouth. If we could have had someone else teaching the class then I would have loved to stay. I had all of her that I could take. Kim understood but was confident enough to stay on the team without me. That was good. She could handle Miss Snotty.

One day I prayed for God to help find some other sport that I would enjoy and love. I really wanted to be involved with something, I just did not know what yet. Through physical education and weight training, I met Mrs. Parr. She would watch me a lot and not say anything. It was like she was studying me. I had a beautiful body then and was quite muscular. I didn't realize it at the time. The guys sure did though. I couldn't keep the guys away from me.

One day Mrs. Parr was talking to me and asked, "Do you like to run?"

I told her, "I love running. I can run forever, I enjoy it so much." She asked if she could meet with me after school, she would like to talk to me more about that. I said, "Sure." I immediately liked her. There was something about her that was very comforting. When I met with her after school, she took me to the back of the school and showed me the track area. As I was looking at the large circle, she asked, "Do you think you can run that?"

I laughed and said, "I could probably run that quite a few times." She wanted to see. I said "OK" and ran around and around the circle as she was timing me. Finally, she told me to stop.

She said, "You would make a good middle and long-distance runner. Would you like to join my track team?"

I said excitedly, "I would love to!"

She said, "I would love to have you and I think you could become a track star with the proper training. I could help you accomplish that. I have been watching you and you are really put together in your mind and body. You can achieve anything you set your mind to, Linda. I say we go for it and make you the star you are." I was pumped up and excited! She was full of good vibe and very positive and cheerful. I had great respect for her because of who she was as a person. She was like an angel sent to me.

Thank you, God, for giving me this opportunity with something I love to do. I had never thought about running for a purpose, I just loved to run! I told her that I would love to join her team. She said that I would have to take constructive criticism and work hard to meet our goals. I told her that I would do whatever it took to accomplish what she had in mind for me.

She said, "Good, then we can go for it and maybe get your college paid for by your talent and great gifts God gave you."

I was happy that she knew God. She told me what I would need a good pair of running shoes, some jogging pants, a comfortable shirt, and shorts for the warm days of running.

I had two days to get this stuff and practice would start after school in a couple of days. I let Kim, Chris, and Theresa know what I had decided. They were happy for me and we went shopping at the sports store in town to get what I needed. My brother Orville gave me the money I needed to get what I needed and supported me doing this. Kim was getting things too and she said we could use this for lifting weights as well. Chris and Kim decided that they would like to check into track as well and see if Mrs. Parr had something they might be good at. Theresa was still not interested but that was OK because we just loved her for who she was. Chris, Kim, Theresa, and I were the four. We spent time with each other every day. We were having the time of our lives. Sometimes we would be so silly that we would laugh so hard and tears would come out of our eyes. I loved school, track, my friends, Mrs. Parr, my teachers, and my home. The Hetterscheids treated me just like I was their daughter and Chris and I were like best friend sisters. I still got to spend time with Orville and his wife Sharon, Kevin and Nancy, and my brother Dale and his friend Tom as well. Life was good! I felt perfectly content and happy. Every day seemed like a good day. I would hear from my mom occasionally but not too much. It was nice to hear her voice when she would call though. I still missed her. Daryl and I would talk sometimes too. I didn't talk to my sister because of her being deaf and living in North Dakota but I would still think about her and her family. As time went on, I became the track star. I could do very well at long distance, the 3000 was my favorite. I also did great at the 800 and the 1500.This man would cheer me on at my track meets, his name was Roger. He was so kind it was just like I had my dad there cheering me on. Roger and I became friends and later found out that he had two sons. Rick was the older one and Randy was still in high school. I knew who Randy was but didn't know Rick. My coach Mrs. Parr and I became very close. She was amazing. She pretty much saw something in me and molded me into what she saw. My weight training instructor was like an army Sargent and he saw something in me too. I was the only girl in the weight training class. He treated me like one of the guys and made me work just as hard as they had to. I wanted to prove to him that I could do this. Nobody in the class seemed to like him but for some reason I did. He also saw potential in me and molded me into what he wanted. He would use me as an example on how to do things correctly to all the guys. He spent extra time with me, pushing me outside of my limits. I listened to everything he said and obeyed him. It wasn't easy, but he really taught me so much. I will forever be thankful.

He matured me mentally without even realizing it. He made me believe in myself. He also made my body very beautiful. I just didn't realize it. Everyone else did. My brothers thought I would end up being a model for playboy or something. When I would wear a swimsuit, the guys would stare too much. It embarrassed me. They would look at me like my head wasn't even attached. When Mrs. Parr would do our measurements, all the girls would circle around me and watch. This would also embarrass me. I couldn't do anything about it so would just have to suck it up. My weight training Instructor saw something in me too. He really liked how I would take constructive criticism and had no problems with discipline. Between him and Mrs.

Parr, I was spending a lot of time lifting weights, exercising, and running. I just kept wanting to do better and better. It was almost addictive. Even though I missed my mom and Daryl, it seemed like I became stronger and stronger every day. I stayed plenty busy enough and enjoyed every day as it came. Every day I felt the urge to do better than the day before. My mom would still call once a month and check in on me. We just never talked about what happened. She knew that I was doing well. My grades were good, and I was in full achievement with track. I loved living with the Hetterscheids. Kim, Chris, Theresa, and I were still the four pack. Daryl had graduated and went into the army, so I didn't hear from him anymore. Mom was still trying to figure out a way to leave Tom. Dale was living with Kevin and Nancy, so we all kept in good touch.

Thanksgiving, Christmas, and Easter were always at my bother Orville's house. We all enjoyed each other's company and became extremely close. My brother Orville would take my friends and me swimming and camping and made sure that we had a great summer. My life was perfect. As a sophomore in high school, guys were starting to get my attention. Only the good-looking ones though. The others made great friends, but I was drawn to good-looking guys. There was quite a few of them in our town. Some had blond hair, and some had brown hair. Too many hunks. Chris and Kim were also noticing guys. Theresa had been noticing for quite a while already. I tried to date a few high school guys, but they seemed to just want to get me alone and then climb all over me, trying to feel things on my body that needed permission to feel. I just wasn't ready to do this, and it scared me that they thought they could, so I would dump them.

The nice ones that I felt comfortable with I just wasn't attracted to. All the good-looking ones that I tried to date were always in a hurry to make out and I really hated that so again I would get rid of them in a hurry.

The other guys in High school that I was attracted to had girlfriends. Maybe I would have to look somewhere else. As time went on, I met a guy named Rick who happened to be Roger's son. He was 22 and I was 16. I thought he was nice and attractive. He was a drummer in a band so that was an edge that I had not experienced. It wasn't long, and we were hanging out with each other a lot. If we weren't with each other than we were on the phone with each other. He was much more mature than the guys in high school and treated me so respectfully. He was a lot of fun and his dad and mom were wonderful people. Chris was dating one of his friends, who was also in the band. Kevin was his name. This worked out well because we could all four hang out with each other. This was great! We were all so happy. Life couldn't get any better! I felt like I was on top of the world.

Chapter 13

The Phone Call That Made Me Cringe

My mom called me. She let me know that she wasn't with Tom anymore and wanted me to move back home. I thought in my head, *You dump me for 3 and ½ years and now suddenly I am supposed to drop everything and come back to you? What are you thinking? How could you ask me to do this?* I didn't want to leave at all. My life was going so perfect, how could she wreck this for me! I felt like I wanted to explode and cry at the same time. Instead, I just listened to her talk. After she was done, I begged her not to do this to me.

She said, "It is time for you to come home. I still have full custody of you. I miss you in my life and now our home is safe for you to come back."

I had no control over this. The Hetterscheids knew what the phone call was about because she had visited with them first. It was out of their hands because they had guardianship of me, but Mom still had full custody of me.

Mrs. Hetterscheid said to me, "Linda, we don't want you to leave either. We enjoy having you in our home and it has been nice for Chris too, but we have to listen to your mother."

I said, "Do you mind if I go for a walk by myself so I can just go think? I really need to clear my mind."

Mr. Hetterscheid said, "We understand and of course you can. We are sorry that this is happening and wish that we could do more, but it sounds like your mom has her mind made up and nobody can change it."

I said, "All of you are like my family and I appreciate you so much! I'm really going to miss all of you so much."

They each gave me a hug before I left the room to go for my walk. I put my running shoes on and decided to go for a run instead. I needed to relieve all this stress and anxiety that was filtering in my mind and body. I ran as fast and furious as I could! I didn't know where I was going, I just kept running. I didn't care where I was going, I kept running and running. I wish that I could just run away and hide. It seemed as though I could run forever and I just wasn't getting tired or out of breath at all. The only reason for me to stop was to blow my nose and wipe my eyes from crying so much! I couldn't stop crying! I felt like the whole world had fallen on me. I couldn't believe my life could change in a blink of an eye like this. As I sobbed and ran, my heart was beating so fast I could hear every beat. I sure wished I could control my own life! I couldn't wait until I turned 18. It was time for me to start heading back because I actually didn't realize how much time had gone by and it was getting to be dusk. I knew that the Hetterscheids would worry if I didn't show up soon. They were so wonderful, I didn't want to add stress to this family. They didn't deserve that, so I went back. When I came inside the house, Chris came up to me and gave me a big hug. I could tell she had been crying too. We were so close and like sisters. This was going to be difficult for us to not live in the same house anymore.

Chris was concerned, she said, "I can't believe this is happening! My parents said that your mom has her mind made up so that really sucks! I guess we will just have to get through this too even though it's going to be so hard." We talked and cried. We were both so devastated.

The next day when I went to school, Mrs. Parr could tell that the life was pulled out of me and how very sad I seemed. She was curious of this sudden change in my attitude. Nothing seemed to matter to me other than feeling abandoned with all I had to do. I talked to Mrs. Parr and explained to her the phone call.

I said to her, "I might as well not even go to practice because I'm going to be leaving anyway. I will have to just leave all of this behind anyway."

But she had an idea to change my mother's view on things. She said, "I can get letters of proof and send them to your mother of how this would be a bad decision on her part. I will let her know that this could affect your life forever and of all you are accomplishing. I will provide your mother with what she needs so she can see how you would lose out on such great opportunity. This needs to be addressed to. A decision like this could take away from scholarships. I think we can change her mind, Linda! I really do! What parent wouldn't want what's best for their child!" Mrs. Parr's big plan was to have me run for the State of Oregon. That was my ambition and plan as well. I wanted this so bad.

It would be an achievement that I could do. She said, "I assure you that your mom will change her mind after seeing the opportunities you have waiting for you. Don't worry, Linda, I am going to help you with this, OK?"

I said, "Thank you, that really means so much to me and thank you for going out of your way for me."

She said, "Things are going to work out!"

Mrs. Parr and many others went out of their way for me to change my mother's views on things. I really appreciated all their help. It was unexpected and brought me hope. We knew that it would take a little time for Mom to get the letters and read them. We decided to carry on as though I wouldn't be leaving until we heard back from her. I let the Hetterscheids know what Mrs. Parr was doing. They were pleased and felt this would change Mom's mind on things. Chris and I were excited and pretty sure that Mom would change her mind.

Things looked brighter and felt better too. I felt at ease and happy again. I had a goal and wished to work hard at making my goal and dream come true. I loved to run and push myself to an extreme. Even though painful and exalting at times I felt good testing myself beyond what I thought I could even do and do better. There were no limits. All I could believe was to do better and keep going with that mentally and physically. I had it in my mind that nobody was going to tell me I can't because I knew I could. It was a challenge and excited me to go beyond my limits to achieve this. The harder I worked the better I felt. Each day I would set a goal on my time and run like you wouldn't believe in order to do what I had to do. I had a strength and power within myself to just go for it!

As the days went by, the phone call finally came but it was not the news I had hoped for. Mom wasn't budging and just let me know that it was time for me to come back home. She said, "You can get involved with things here and do the same thing you're doing, just in a different state. Everything will be fine, Linda."

How deeply sad and betrayed I felt. I had no control of my life. Mom suddenly had all control. I felt a lot of resentment towards her and suddenly hated my life. I couldn't believe this was happening. I begged and pleaded with Mom, but nothing was working for me. I felt very angry inside but had to listen anyway. She was my mother. I just had to listen.

She said, "I will let you at least stay until school is over. Daryl will drive out and get you. We will talk more before then. I can't wait to see you, Linda! I sure miss you and love you."

I said "I love you too" in a depressed tone. I was glad I could stay a little longer but not much. School would be over too soon. Sometimes things are out of our control and this was one of those times for me. I had to enjoy each day I could with all that I could because it wouldn't be long, and I would have to leave. Soon the day came when I had to say goodbye to all my friends, family, and many special people. There were a lot of tears and I did not want to get in the car and leave. My brother Sargent Daryl was as strait-laced as you could get. I really had a tough time getting in the car and before you knew it, we were driving down the road.

Things were quiet. He didn't say anything, and I didn't have anything to say to him. I felt so sad thinking of where I was going. Every thought led to horror. *Please God help me! Get me out of this!* The way Daryl was driving was very annoying. He drove like an old man. He seemed to be driving so slowly. I finally told him to please drive faster so cars would stop passing us. He told me that he is obeying the law. He had a perfect record and wanted to keep it that way. He said that he wanted to go into law enforcement and help keep people safe. *Oh great! Now I have Mr. Cop on my hands that won't budge over the speed limit!*

"Daryl, we have a long way to go, can't you please try and get us there faster. This is going to take forever the way you're driving. I am pretty sure that cops drive much faster than this."

He told me to just take a nap instead of telling him how he should drive. I never drove the speed limit and enjoyed driving fast so we argued a lot. He was so serious. What had happened to my brother? Did the army do this? They must have sucked all the fun right out of him. I turned the music on and he got mad at me for doing that.

He said that it was a distraction.

"Well, the way you are driving is a distraction and you are going to cause an accident with all these people passing."

He said, "I think you are just crabby and taking it out on me. You should be happy that you finally get to come home and be with Mom."

"Happy? Are you nuts? What is there to be happy about? All those letters that my track coach sent Mom, she is messing up everything I worked so hard to achieve. I could have got my College paid for and possibly even ended up in the Olympics. Happy? I must leave my boyfriend and friends just because she suddenly wants me home. Happy that I will live in the same town as Tom and possibly run into Rick again too. You guys are wrecking my life!"

"Linda, I didn't know anything about the letters. Mom got away from Tom and you knew that when she could make the home safe for you that you would be coming back."

"Daryl, it took her three years. Excuse me if I feel unimportant to her."

"Oh, Linda stop it! Mom loves you and misses you very much. She needs you."

"Where was she when I needed her? She sent me off and stayed with Tom for three years and now she wants me to just drop my life and be with her?"

Daryl said, "Linda, I am sorry. I know you're hurting. Please just try and make the best of things. One of the reasons I am going into law enforcement is because of what you have gone through."

I started to cry and told Daryl that he would make a great cop. "I know you will help many and protect people."

He asked if I wanted to drive for a while. Finally, we could get a move on! He stopped the car to put in gas and I got in the driver seat.

"Linda, please don't speed."

I drove the speed limit for a little bit and noticed he went to sleep. I put on the radio and kept it down. I'm not sure what got into me, but I decided to catch up for lost time. Since he was sleeping, he wouldn't even know. I was passing cars and even some that had passed us. If he could just stay sleeping, I could get us there. As I was driving, I started to remember how Daryl and I would do things together and have so much fun. My heart felt better thinking about the good times we had together. I had good memories to think about and it made my mood better too. When Daryl woke up, he thanked me for driving while he got some sleep. He said he could drive the rest of the way. He told me to try and get some sleep. I let him know that I was sorry for being so crabby and that I loved him. He said that he loved me too, and not to worry and everything will work out. "Linda, I will always protect you," he said.

I thanked him and said that I needed it. "Where we are going has so many horrible memories and this is very hard on me." I let him know that I would be strong and do it, but I was not looking forward to it. I said, "I miss Dad so much! I really wish he was here. I feel so lost and lonely without him."

Daryl let me know that Dad really loved me so much that he used to wish Dad would treat him the way Dad treated me. He said that Dad and he were very close and after I was born, things changed. "You became Dad's life. Mom was even jealous of you. We loved you though and all of us loved taking care of you. You listened so well, and boy did you ever love Jesus! It was neat." He laughed and said, "Remember when you were in 4th grade and stood up in front of your class and said you were going to be President of the United States of America. That was so funny! Dad didn't laugh, he said you would make a great president. Whatever Linda does, she will put everything she has into it! It's just the way she is. She loves to help people. I believe she can be anything she sets her mind to."

I said, "I remember that, and I changed my mind. I am not sure what I want to be. A lot of things come to my mind. I guess I will figure it out sooner or later."

Daryl said, "I understand. There is a lot of choices to make and it takes time to figure it out. Whatever you decide, you will do great!" He said, "You should get some sleep, you will feel better if you do."

I put my seat back and it didn't take long, and I was sleeping. When I woke up, we were in front of Mom's house. She came running outside with a big smile on her face and her arms wide open. She gave me a huge hug and said, "Welcome home. The house hasn't been the same without you. I have missed you so much and have been waiting for this day to come. You are my daughter! Nobody can ever replace you. I am so sorry for everything you went through because of me. I truly am sorry. Now our home is safe for you and me. Tom is out of the picture. I wish I had never married him. Let's go inside I have been cooking and I'm sure you both must be hungry."

When I walked into the kitchen, I realized the last time I was in this kitchen was a horrible memory. I felt sick to my stomach thinking about it! I told Mom that I was going to put my stuff in my room and maybe lay down. I wasn't feeling very good.

She asked if I was OK.

I said, "Yes, I just feel a little sick to my stomach."

She said if I needed anything to let her know and asked if I would like a little 7up. I said sure, so she got me one. I said thank you. She said she hoped that I feel better.

When I went to my room, it was like a dark cloud. I had visions of Tom trying to get into my bedroom. I had visions of me climbing out my window and how scared I was. All these horrible visions kept me feeling sick to my stomach. Suddenly, I had to throw up. I ran to the bathroom and threw up. Daryl came running in and asked if I was OK. I told him that my nerves must be making me sick. He got my 7up for me and a wash cloth. I told him thank you and went back to my room.

Mom wanted to know if I was OK. I told her that I was fine, I was just going to lay down for a little bit. While laying down, I remembered all the bad things that I went through. If I could just shut my brain off and stop thinking. I then prayed that Jesus would please give me peace and take away these memories and make them please go away. I kept saying over and over please Jesus please. I must have repeated myself 50 times or more and then finally felt relaxed and better. I thanked him over and over and let him know how much I loved him. I got up and went out to the living room. Mom and Daryl were watching TV. I sat down and joined them. Mom asked if I was feeling better. I told her that I was feeling much better.

She said, "Oh good."

They were watching a funny show. It made all of us laugh. I don't remember the name of it, but it felt good to laugh with Mom and Daryl. I guess I did miss them. I didn't realize it.

Being around them was nice even though I really missed Oregon already. I missed my boyfriend, family, and friends. Chris and I were with each other every day. How I missed her so much. *OK, I need my mind to shut off again.* Even though I was watching TV, my mind was thinking of everything in Oregon. As time went on, Daryl was living in Fargo and got married to Cheryl. They were meant to be, so a wedding was no surprise to anyone. It was just Mom and me. She didn't spend much time at home. She spent a lot of time with her friend Vicky. I felt alone again.

I started to hang out with my old friends. They all smoked cigarettes and drank a lot. I tried to drink with them, but it was hard to keep up with them. I kept doing this and became a little reckless. I was so angry and hurt that I just didn't care anymore. When I called my boyfriend in Oregon, he told me that he found a girl Julie and they ended up getting together. He said he was sorry. He also said that he just couldn't handle long distance relationships. My heart was broken. I cried so hard. I decided heck with it, I might as well go party with my friends. I ended up getting careless and making out with quite a few different guys. I would make out with them and break their hearts. I had no interest in having a boyfriend and I didn't care about any of their feelings. I didn't care if I hurt them. It didn't matter. I think I turned numb. I was so sick of people hurting me that I lost all trust in people, especially men. I stayed having this attitude until one day Mom said she didn't like how unhappy I was, and she would let me move back to Oregon, but I would have to stay with Kevin and Nancy and go to school there. I said, "Fine with me!" She was never home anyway so at least I would be with people that cared. She argued with me for a little bit and then left. I was in no mood for anyone that day, so I stayed home by myself and talked to myself too. I started to pack my things and clean the house because I had to get rid of this bad energy somehow. My Uncle Harley and Aunt Karen stopped by. It was nice to see them. They were so sweet. That changed my mood. They were like a couple of angels. They didn't stay long but it sure was nice to have such good company. Harley was my mom's brother, so he was sorry that they missed seeing her but told me to tell her that they stopped by. They just felt like going for a drive. Harley was funny. He always made me laugh. He had the nicest smile and Karen was always smiley and kind. They were true love. They always seemed so happy. I hoped someday I would have that. They were a perfect example of a successful marriage. How lucky they were to have such love. Deep down inside, I really wanted love. Somebody to just show me love. I missed my dad so much. Mom was so lucky to have him for a husband. He treated her so good. After he died, it was hard to understand why she got in a relationship so fast. She should have waited.

I was so glad that I was finally getting out of there and couldn't wait to go back to Oregon. I turned on the TV and flipped through the channels. I liked 'Three is Company' and decided on that. Jack and Mr. Furley would make me laugh and so would Janet and Chrissy. Of course, I couldn't forget Mr. and Mrs. Roper. They were all funny. I loved this show.

I was laughing all by myself, but I couldn't help it. I watched three more episodes. Mom and Vickey came home. They were being loud and silly. They were tuned up. Vicky was a lot of fun and I must say she made me laugh a lot. She was such a goof ball. Mom and she decided to go uptown for a while. I thought to myself that they really didn't need to drink anymore because they were already tuned up plenty. *Oh well, I guess I will watch some more TV*, I thought. I saw Johnny Carson was on so decided to watch that. I really enjoyed Johnny, he was great. I found it fun how he would have animals on his show. That was always fun to watch.

It was getting late and suddenly, I felt like a mother to my mom and Vicky. Even though they are much older and wiser than me, I felt wiser and older than them. I was worried about them, but I had to let it go. *I decided to just go to sleep. They probably won't get home until the bar closes anyways. Who knows what they will do afterwards? I just needed to stop worrying about them. They are adults if they need me, they will call. They certainly know where I am.* I fell asleep and woke up to a lot of noise. I went to see what was going on and it was Mom having a hard time walking. I helped her get into bed and then I went back to bed. When I got up in the morning, Mom was still in bed. I decided to make her breakfast because she probably wasn't feeling very well after last night. After I got breakfast made, I went into her room. She smelled like booze. *Ugh!*

"Mom, good morning."

She got up and said, "Where is my car?"

She went running outside in a panic and her car was in the driveway. I couldn't help but to laugh. It was obvious she didn't remember driving home, so she shouldn't have had been driving. When she came back in the house, I had her plate fixed. She sat down at the table and thanked me. I asked her if she wanted some orange juice, but she said she would rather have coffee. Soon Vicky was knocking at the door. I let her in and she smelled the house and said I came just in time. I dished her up a plate of what I was going to eat but figured she needed it more than me. I told her that the coffee was brewing and should be done soon. She told me that I looked pretty without any makeup on. She said that I didn't need all that make up.

I laughed and said, "That is your opinion."

She said, "I am telling you the truth, Linda."

I just smiled and said, "Thank you, Vicky."

Mom said that breakfast was good.

Vicky said, "You are going to be a good wife to someone, Linda."

I said, "I don't even want to get married. Men are the last things on my mind right now."

Vicky laughed and said, "You will change your mind when Mr. Charming comes along."

I said, "None of them charm me. They're all a bunch of jerks."

"Oh my! Someone has a bad attitude today!"

I asked Mom when I was going to Oregon. She said that I would leave in a couple of days.

I said, "OK, I will pack some more stuff."

Vicky said, "It's too bad you are going back, it's been nice having you around."

I looked at her and said, "Don't worry, I will keep in touch."

She said that I better.

I went to my room. I hoped they wouldn't go out again tonight. They probably would though. They seemed to go out every night. *It will probably be Johnny Carson and I again. Well, I guess I will be in Oregon soon, so mise well just let it be.* I could hear them laughing a lot but just didn't feel like seeing what was so funny. I was feeling a little sad and wanted to be alone. I didn't feel like being around anyone but was hoping I could see Daryl before moving back to Oregon again. I felt like I didn't really have anything left here to stay for. I was feeling guilty about some of the choices I had made being here. I wasn't sure what got into me, and I didn't think I cared at the time but now I did.

The guys I made out with were my old classmate friends and didn't deserve how I took advantage of them. I needed to just get out of here because I didn't want to face any of them, I felt so ashamed. I decided to just stay by myself until I left. I was too scared to go apologize. In my mind it was bothering me though. I knew everyone made mistakes, but I felt like I was the only one. I was beating myself up pretty good, so I don't think anyone could match that. I wish I could just leave then. I just wanted to go home. I knew Oregon was my home. I felt good there and loved everything. The scenery was much better too. The ocean was close for my time away and I truly loved the ocean. The sound of the waves while walking on the beach was like therapy for me. Some people pay for it and I got it free from God. He knew the effect this would have on some people and I was one of them. As I started to think of all the good memories in Oregon, my mind stopped beating up on myself. I had something good to focus on and look forward to. I couldn't wait to see everyone again, especially Chris. I missed her so much. We were good at keeping each other happy. We could hang out for hours and not get bored with each other. I started smiling thinking of the great memories we had. We just never got sick of each other even though we were glued to each other. That is true friendship. I will always cherish the love I have for Chris and keep in touch with her forever. She knew everything about me, bad and good. She never judged me and always was there for me no matter what.

After a couple of days of getting ready for the move, the time approached for me to go back to Oregon and say goodbye to Mom once again. I did get to see Daryl and he gave me the biggest strongest hug. It reminded me of Dad. He told me to go be a champion and show the world what I was made of. I was so delighted that he came to see me off. Daryl was a great guy. He was one of the most intelligent men I had met other than my dad. I guess all my brothers and sister were smart people. I felt lucky to be blessed with such amazing siblings. Dale was the funny one of the family. He was a prankster and loved to make people laugh. Kevin and Orville were both about success. Elaine was a wonderful wife and mother. I was still trying to figure out who I was.

There were a lot of times I thought about what I was going to remember that seemed so important to remember at the very beginning. I also wondered if I was supposed to even remember any of it. I just knew that my dad had told me not to talk about it and figured he knew what was best for me. I still thought about it a lot though. I wondered what that place was, and I couldn't forget about how great I felt there. It was awfully hard to feel that good here in this world. When I got to Oregon and moved into Kevin and Nancy's place, I felt a little scared. They were wonderful and treated me so good. Nancy and I became very close. She would call me on anything I did wrong but understood me. She would let me know that she was my age once and understood me. I loved how truthful she was with me. My brother Kevin was so supportive to me and gave me and showed me love. My brother Dale was so fun to be around. He always brought laughter no matter what was going on. He really loved me and showed it in so many ways. My brother Orville was so protective of me just like a father and sometimes it would get annoying. He watched me and always knew what I was doing.

I knew he just loved me to pieces and would do anything to keep me safe, but his worry and protection seemed so annoying at times that sometimes we would argue a bit. I don't think he ever wanted me to date. All my brothers thought I would be a model, but I didn't want any part of that. I didn't think of myself as beautiful. My self-esteem was taken from me after Tom's experience and I was not sure how to get it back. After losing my dad that was a big piece missing in my life. My mom choosing Tom deprived me of feeling loved. I felt like a lost child skipping the things out of my head that I didn't want to remember so running and working out were an escape for me.

I knew I would be going to a much bigger school. This was a scary thought. Kevin said I would need to work and help pitch in financially. He had a job lined up for me in a berry field. It would be long hours and hard work but knew I could do it. It was a start and I had to start somewhere. My first day of work was so awful. I was the only girl and all the men I worked with only knew Spanish. I didn't have a clue what they were saying, and they couldn't understand me neither.

Sometimes they would speak Spanish and look at me and laugh. I just worked and ignored them as best as I could. It was uncomfortable for me though. When it was finally time to get off work and go home, I was beat.

Kevin wanted to know how things went so I told him. He said I needed to be strong and just work hard. I said that I would. I continued doing this for a couple of weeks, but it was so terrible. Sometimes snakes would come through on the belt I was working on and mice too. That was my last draw. I just couldn't handle this job and was done with it. When I went home, I told Kevin that I wanted to find a different job. This was too hard on me.

He told me to go ahead. I walked down the street and wasn't even gone an hour and got a job at this place called King's Table. They wanted me to start that night, but I needed to have black dress pants and a white shirt.

I was so excited, I ran home as fast as I could and told Kevin the good news. Unfortunately, he didn't believe me that I got a job that quickly. I promised him with all my heart, but he said, "You haven't even been gone an hour. Nobody gets a job that fast."

I said, "Well, I must walk to Fred Meyer's and get a pair of black dress pants and a white shirt." I headed to Fred Meyers, got what I needed, and came back and got ready for work.

When I was leaving, he told me good luck and smiled and said, "You amaze me."

When I got to work and was shown what to do, I fell in love with the employees, my manager, and boss. They were all wonderful. This made me so happy. I loved my new job, and everyone spoke English. I didn't have to deal with mice and snakes anymore. I appreciated that more than words could say. My life was getting better and I was full of joy once again. One of the employees named Cherie was very fun. She and I would be in the same school and same grade.

That was so great to know that I would be able to start school knowing someone.

We became instant friends and started to hang out after work too. There was a very good looking and charming guy named Lance and we had an immediate attraction between us. He was so funny and so good-looking. We also started hanging out together. Things were just great. As time went on, Lance and I became more than just friends and became friends with benefits. He had a friend named Mike that I instantly liked and became my buddy too. I could talk to Mike about anything and he was always there for me like a friend should be. Through Mike I met more friends and soon we had our own little gang. It was Mike, Lance, Bobby, Jay, Cherie, and I. Bobby was also very good looking and so much fun. He and I developed a very close friendship. When I met his family, I instantly fell in love with all of them. Bobby had great taste in clothing and always smelled good and looked good. We got along like best friends. He never tried anything funny with me and I just loved hanging out with him. He was very energetic like me and made everything fun. My brother Orville decided to buy me the ugliest car I had ever seen in my life. It was a gremlin. I was embarrassed driving such an ugly car. When I would have my friends with me, we would laugh at how ugly the car was. I didn't have it very long and gave it back to Orville and told him that I would buy my own car but thanked him for trying to help me out.

He laughed and said, "It wasn't too ugly, was it?"

I laughed and said, "At stoplights, I duck so nobody can see me."

At least he understood and was nice about it. That day I bought a 1969 red bug. It was adorable. I loved this car. I fixed it up to make it cuter. Cherie had a blue Honda civic. It was cute too. Her dad loved bugs and would love to work on them too. That was a good thing considering I owned one. It was so fun to drive on the curvy roads of Oregon. Chris would stop by and see me, and I would also visit her and my old friends that I used to hang around with. The day came when it was time for me to start school. The school had so many people, security, and nobody even knew that I was a new kid. That was the first time that ever happened to me. I liked my principal a lot.

Cherie and I would meet up on our lunch breaks. As I was driving my bug and trying to hurry back to school, I got pulled over for speeding. It didn't take me long to get a ticket. I was so scared to tell Kevin and Nancy. I talked to my manager at work and she said she would go to court with me and help me out. I had to have an adult with me. That worked. I had to write about speeding and how important it was not to speed and hand it to the Court office when finished. That was what they decided so I didn't have to pay a fine. I learned not to speed on lunch break anymore but still would sometimes in other areas. I was more alert though to watch for cops. My bug was a fun car to drive. Orville bought new tires for it which was so nice of him to do. Now I stayed busy between work, school, family, and friends. Time was going by fast. I didn't have time for sports even though I wanted to be involved. I had to keep working to pay Kevin and Nancy rent. Kevin, Dale, and I would go to the coast and go crabbing. That was a lot of fun and yummy for the tummy. Sometimes my friends and I would go to the coast and just have fun. Lance and I were not boyfriend and girlfriend, but we had a lot of chemistry. That was something we just had. He was a great guy, we both just didn't take our relationship any further. It was fun flirting with each other and being so close though. I will always cherish that.

I helped the school in the office too. They eventually got me a job at Valley Motors. Most people know it as Mercedes Benz. I would work there after school every day. My brother Orville was very pleased with me getting that job. He would tell me to hang in there and I would have a job for life. It wasn't the best job for me though. I liked my old job better. There were times I felt like quitting because of some issues but hung in there. My brother Orville also put it in my head to never quit a job unless you have a better one lined up. I wasn't good at sitting, I liked to be physical and moving so this was different for me. There was also some flirtation by guys much older than me that I didn't care for at all. I would get tired of that and it made me feel uncomfortable. It's life though, if you're a female, it's just life. I was smart but still naive. I tried to avoid anything uncomfortable. I tried to stay strong and just do my job. I pictured things better than this in my head, but it was a learning experience for me, that's for sure. As time went on and passed, I learned a lot of things.

Now it was my senior year in high school. I still was hanging with the same friends. When it came to graduation, my mom and Daryl both drove out to be there for me. My neighbor Larae told me that she could get me a job working for Trionic Alarm Company. It was dispatching, Alarm Center, a telephone board to connect calls through and much more exciting things as well. The pay was great, and this was quite a job for an 18-year-old to have. I decided to go for it. Larae trained me in. It was a very busy job. A lot to learn, and fast paced. I loved it! The people that I worked with were terrific. This was the best job ever. I had so much responsibility in my hands. I learned quickly and then was on my own on the night shifts. I was in a highly secured building. Salem Merchant Patrol was always driving by and checking on me. I dispatched for them as well as many others. It was comforting to know that they were constantly checking on me while I was alone. I didn't feel alone knowing this. This job had many benefits and a very good income. I was making the money that forty-year-old people would make. I was doing very well at such a young age. I got my own apartment and Cherie and a couple other friends would stay with me a lot. My place was always full of friends when I was home. It was work and slumber parties at my place all the time. I was never bored, that is for sure. Sometimes my brother Orville would stop by when I was sleeping with a crockpot full of meat, potatoes, and carrots. He would plug it in, so I would wake up to the smell. I loved how he would think of me and surprise me with his gifts of love. My friends did too.

Food was always a good thing at this age in life. Food and fun were priority. I still had my old friends too, so I introduced my new friends to my old friends and made it work. I ended up getting a roommate. She was good at first but became a problem later. Bobby, Cherie, Jay, and I ended up finding a nicer place to live and we could all share expenses. This was good because we were all working and could pitch in. Jay and Bobby shared a bedroom and Cherie and I shared a bedroom. We stayed organized with responsibilities and made it work for quite some time. Drama started happening. Especially between Jay and Bobby. They acted like they were a married couple that didn't get along most of the time. Cherie and I were fine. We tried to stay out of the drama, but it was hard when we lived in it. Soon we realized that this wasn't working out and I moved back with my brother Kevin again until I could get situated. Things had changed with him and Nancy too. They seemed to both be so different. They were partying a lot and not getting along like they used to. The many people that would stop by looked like bad people. I wasn't sure what was going on but knew it wasn't good. It didn't take long, and Kevin was on work men's comp for a back injury. Nancy and Kevin decided to get a divorce. It was sad to see that happen. Nancy and I always got along so good. I couldn't figure out what had happened. It was their decision though and I had to set my personal feelings aside. I didn't like all the strange people coming over all hours of the night. It was odd and didn't make sense to me.

The company I was working for had been bought out by Pace Security and interviewed my coworkers and I to see who they would keep working for them. I was one of the few chosen. This was a much bigger company and much more money. I was so excited about this opportunity and liked the new owner. He was very motivated. I was working very long hours during the transition. The new office was in Lake Oswego and the old office was still going. I was working both places and very long hours. The drive back and forth was also putting on quite a few miles. I wasn't home much. I really didn't have a lot of time for family or friends with this job change. I was getting plenty of overtime. I was working in the Portland office too. My manager was in love with himself. I immediately was disgusted with that. Him and I were so opposite in personalities. My heart was caring and loving, his was not. He was my manager, so I had to just put up with him. The other people I worked with were wonderful. I worked with all men, but it wasn't uncomfortable.

These guys were respectful and good guys. I enjoyed working with them. We stayed plenty busy but still had time to visit in between calls coming in. Again, I had so much to learn but picked up fast and was thankful for that. The building in Lake Oswego was huge. They scanned our eye and that is how we would enter in and out of this building. Things changed for me rapidly and now I really felt like an adult. Work was my life now. When I would come home to Kevin, he was spending a lot of time with this other guy. I liked his new friend because he seemed so smart and good for Kevin. As time went on, I learned that these two were in the cocaine business.

They were dealing with some big shots. I was working so much that I really couldn't try and figure this out. I had to take care of me. When I finally got some normal hours instead of constantly working overtime, I felt human again. The pay checks were huge. My hard work paid off. I was making more money than my brothers and I was much younger than them. This was a good thing. I could grow with this company and stick with them for who knows how long. Kevin was going through some tough times in his life. The divorce was hard on him and financially he was used to doing well. That all changed now because he was waiting for a settlement with workman's comp and the divorce and credit card debt was draining. I was helping him out and trying to keep him positive rather than negative. He and his partner in crime were always together and I got to know his partner and family very well. We built trust with each other over time. His partner said I was an observer. I didn't say much but observed everything. I think I had always been that way. Nothing slipped by me and I loved to watch and learn new things. His partner taught me how to make glass pipes. It was so interesting how fire and glass worked. It was like meditation. I loved doing this and became very creative. It was like a hobby. Sometimes I would get off work and they were both so high that they would have me count their money and drive for them. I didn't even realize that knowing what they were doing was a crime too. I was so naive to this. I always thought that I was just helping them. I knew what they were doing was against the law. I wasn't sure what to feel about that because of how smart these guys were. As time went on, they were using a lot more than they should have. They shouldn't have had been using at all. Realistically, they shouldn't be doing anything they were doing. His partner had a wife and two kids. She didn't use, and she was a wonderful wife and mother. She accepted what they were doing and was older and wiser than I, so I figured I should just accept it too. I would give her breaks and watch the kids for her and feed the guys. I liked her a lot. Their kids were fun to watch and play with. As time went on, things were getting more careless. They were using more and acting paranoid. Whenever their bosses would call, I was never to know their names and take a message. They would refer to themselves as shithead or something weird like that. I would get so nervous when talking to them because I knew they were big stuff. They didn't say much over the phone and had code words that I didn't understand. I would just relay the messages. I always respected this and didn't ask any questions. The less I knew the better. Orville met me privately and said he didn't like what was going on and wanted me to get out of that house. He said he thought we should tell our cousin Larry everything that was going on with Kevin and his partner.

Larry had been working for law enforcement for several years and was very highly ranked. I was afraid for Kevin and his partner. I was afraid for all of them. I didn't know what to do. Orville begged me to come with him to meet Larry. I just couldn't do it. I was hanging tight with Bobby and his family at the time. Bobby got a job offer in Alaska and offered for me to come with. I said no at the time because I didn't want to leave my job. I told Orville this and he said, "Go. I will even pay for your plane ticket and bring you to the airport."

I talked to Kevin and his partner and warned them. I also let them know that I was moving to Alaska and that I missed Bobby. I asked them to please be careful and listen to what I told them. Even though I didn't feel comfortable about turning them in, deep down I felt that Orville would probably still follow through with it. I did the best I could at warning them, but I think they were into deep with the big wigs.

Chapter 14

North to Alaska

I said my goodbyes and Orville put me on the plane; I loved the flight. When almost landing, Alaska looked so very beautiful, it was like I had landed in Paradise. When I got off the plane, Bobby's cousin picked me up. She was so welcoming and kind. I liked her immediately. She let Bobby and me stay with her and her family until we got our own place. Life went well while living in Alaska. Bobby and I were so happy. We met so many wonderful people. We both had good jobs and made good money. I found out the news that I wasn't expecting at all. I was carrying a child. Now we had something to really think about. This is a big life change for both of us. I was so happy about how Bobby reacted. He was so happy, and we called his sister right away to tell her the good news. I also called Orville to share the news with him as well. This was so great! I immediately fell in love with my baby in me. As friends and family got involved more with talking with Bobby, the cheer was gone. They all were talking to me about abortion or adoption, including Bobby. My heart felt so hurt by this.

How could everyone feel this way? I thought Bobby was happy and going to support this. Suddenly, I felt betrayed and very alone. I had so much to think about and now I was so scared. When I finally figured things out and came up with a decision to keep this baby and no talking me out of it, then soon life really changed for me. I had never felt this kind of love before. This was something only a mother could experience. My body was changing. It was interesting how so many things changed with me and my body to prepare for this precious baby. Even though I was still a child and had a lot of growing up to do, this was an everlasting lifetime changing experience for me and was meant to be. As I continued going on and went through some hard times with some things that crossed my path with Bobby, he got scared and left me. He didn't tell me that he was leaving. One day I came home to an empty home. My heart was broken once again. My tears could have filled a bath tub. Now I was alone. I had to get through this somehow. I needed to just be strong. *I must be strong for the baby. Please God, please give me the strength I need to do this.* A friend of mind showed up at my place and could tell something was wrong. I am sure it was obvious with my puffed-up eyes and empty home. We talked, and she must have been God sent. She told me to come live with her and her boyfriend, that they had room. This way I wouldn't have to be alone and could save money instead of spending more for rent. That did sound like a good idea considering Bobby and I split everything. I had nothing but memories of him plastered all over our home and needed to get away from it and move forward with my life. As time went on, my doctor informed me that I would have to deliver this child in Anchorage. He didn't want my risky complications with my history of not to bear a child and thought it would be wise to have a specialist involved. I was told as a teenager that I wouldn't be able to have children because of a lot of reasons. I would have to move to Anchorage because I couldn't afford to fly back and forth for doctoring. Now I had a lot more to think about. I would have to leave my job, find a place to live, find a job... The people I was living with were not getting along and having their own problems. My friend had been talking to me about leaving him and that maybe she and I could get a place to live. I was thinking in my head whether this could work or not.

The reality of things would be that she would also need to get a job. That would make two of us instead of one and this was in the winter when people were not hiring and laying people off. I didn't know what to do. *God, please help me with this. I give it to you because I just don't know what to do. Please, God, please take this stress away and help make things safe for my baby.*

God is amazing! That evening, my friend got a phone call from her mother. While she was on the phone, I was watching a commercial of all these different advertisements for food that I had not seen since I moved to Alaska. My mouth was watering. I took out the garbage and it was so cold and icky outside. I wished I could be in the sun right at that moment. When I got back in the house, Lori wanted to tell me something. She was smiling and very excited!

I joked and said, "What? Are you going to take winter away and bring me the sun? Are you going to bring Pizza Hut to me? Are you going to give me a new life?"

She laughed and said, "Yes to all of those!"

I said, "What do you mean?"

Chapter 15

Prayers Answered, Love of God

She let me know that her mother called, and they are in process of buying a house but were locked up in their condo for six months. We could live rent-free in a very nice condo while we looked for work. It would be in Glendive, Arizona. I started laughing and jumping up and down with joy! We were both so excited! We started packing right away and scheduling a flight.

My goodness, Thank you, God, my most Heavenly Father. Thank you so much!

We stayed to finish a week at work and give our jobs' notice. We then flew into Phoenix, Arizona, and the sun was shining. How good this felt. Lori's Mom and stepdad were wonderful people. They were excited and thankful to get in their new home. We were also excited to begin a new life. The next day Lori and I went and filled out applications. We also took advantage of all the food we hadn't seen for a very long time. I also made a doctor's appointment right away. This was a good day. I could not believe the weather, fruit trees, fresh lemons, and how so many things were in walking distance. It was incredible. This felt good and right. The memories of Bobby were gone now. This was meant to be, and God chose it. The next day Target called me for an interview. I figured out from trying to put in applications that my pregnancy was becoming an issue getting a job because of risk and insurance reasons. I had to make money to take care of this baby. I decided to wear bigger clothing to cover up my belly to see if I could just get a job. I went to the interview.

It went very well. They seemed to like me and set me up with two more interviews. I went to them as well. Everything went very well, and I got hired. I would start training the next day. *OH goodness, this is wonderful!* Target was in walking distance too. I was so full of glee and so happy! I let Lori and her parents know the good news. They all were happy for me. Being as I was six months pregnant I knew that Target would find out sooner or later, but I had better make as much money as I could, just in case they would have to let me go when they figured things out. I never lied to them. I just didn't tell them and discretely covered my proof up.

Our home was beautiful with colors of peach carpet and white walls. It had a lot of living space. Lori let me have the master bedroom with a huge bathroom and lots of room. She felt it was the right thing to do being as I would be having a baby soon. She and Courtney also had a very big bedroom with plenty of room. This place was so comforting, and we felt very safe. When we would go to the swimming pool and hot tub area, we would meet others who lived there. Everyone seemed so nice and welcoming. As time went on, Lori went through jobs and would get fired for some reason. It took her a month and half before she got a job. I was paying for everything. Her parents were so disappointed and would vent to me.

They couldn't believe that I got a job so quickly and she didn't. They were pretty upset that she wouldn't hold on to a job. Lori had to figure things out for her own. I understood her parent's frustration though. She was my best friend though and I had to keep her positive. I loved her and her daughter very much and they were there for me when I needed someone. I appreciated her friendship and would always be there for her as well. She wasn't the most motivated person and some people are that way. She was beautiful and reminded me of Farah Faucet. Men were very attracted to her. She stayed busy with the men. She could be a bit lazy with cleaning, so I would try to just take care of that as much as possible. I got a phone call from my brother Kevin. He got in a lot of trouble. The law enforcement finally busted him and his partner. They both had to leave the state of Oregon and never come back. He had nowhere to go so asked if he could come stay with me for a while. I told him that if he didn't do any drugs he could, because no drugs were allowed in my home. He said that he would respect that, and he never wanted to touch drugs again. "Believe me, Linda, I have learned my lesson." He asked if Dale could come with. I told him that they would have to get jobs and they could stay until they get on their feet again. He was so thankful! He said that he tried everyone he could think of before calling me. They were going to leave that night.

I looked forward to helping them. We are a very close family. Kevin and Dale both helped me when I was going through a tough time, so now, I was willing to help them out. I was keeping in good touch with my mom. She also wanted to come out and help me, so that I wouldn't be stressed. She felt the need to stay with me for a while, so she could be a part of my baby on the way to birth. She said that I needed a mother and it was time for her to be one. She looked forward to being a grandmother. Any way she could help, she would like to be there for me. I was so glad she offered, because I really could use a mom to just be with me. Lori had no problem with the company coming. She was excited! Kevin and Dale kept calling me and letting me know where they were. They sounded so happy instead of in distress. That made me feel happy too. The next day they arrived and got settled in. They were so excited about the pool and hot tub. I couldn't use the hot tub but enjoyed swimming. Target would call me when anyone would call in sick. I would take the extra hours gladly. The more money I could make, the better for me. I worked in many different departments, so it was a lot of fun to learn new things. They were so wonderful to work for and realized I was pregnant as time went on. They weren't mad or upset. They were actually very supportive.

My mother had hurt her back, playing basketball at a very young age. She suffered this pain for many years. She had back surgery done, but it still didn't help her. When she came to stay with me, she was in much less pain. She thought that maybe the heat helped her and also the hot tub as well. My brother Kevin started to go to college and my brother Dale got a job working at Dillard's. Everything was going well for everyone. Lori and Dale became boyfriend and girlfriend. I started nesting and getting ready for my baby to come. Our home was very neat, organized, and sparkly clean. I even alphabetically ordered all my canned goods. Mom was the one that said I was nesting. I couldn't see my feet in the shower any more. I felt uncomfortable and wanted this baby to come out. I decided that I wanted natural childbirth, even though I had specialists involved with my pregnancy and let me know that may not be able to happen. I was very set on doing this and nothing was changing my mind. All the employees at Target figured I would have a boy. Only one thought I would have a girl. Some of the customers loved coming in and watching my tummy.

My baby was very active and would put on quite the show. I had so much support from so many people. I even had men to offer to be my boyfriend and take care of this child. I didn't accept any offers. I knew that I was very capable of doing this myself. I didn't want anything to do with men at the time and had been hurt enough. I didn't plan on ever having a boyfriend or a husband. I wanted to just concentrate on my baby and myself. I didn't have trust for men and tried to avoid them. I couldn't believe that they were attracted to me even though I was ready to pop. I figured they must be desperate to try and date a pregnant woman.

Soon the big day came while I was at work, I began having contractions. Everyone in Target began to panic. I was telling everyone to settle down. I called Lori to come and get me, that it was time. She was also in a panic. She drove like a crazy woman. She even almost ran into someone walking across the street. *Dear, Lord please get me to the hospital safely.* When we arrived, Lori called my brothers and Mom. Everyone came in the room with me. I was trying everything I could to handle the pain. The specialist said the baby was turned and I needed to take some pain medication. I would not and told him so. Another specialist came and talked with me and said I had to. This was dangerous for me and the baby. I still refused to take anything. I said I wanted to do this naturally, not on drugs. Finally, they gave me a shot through my IV without a choice. I am not sure what they gave me, but I got higher than a kite. I invited everyone to come in the delivery room with me and everyone kept laughing at me. I don't remember what I was saying and doing that was so funny. They had never seen me this way, so couldn't help but to laugh. Kevin and Lori stayed in the delivery room with me, while the others waited in the waiting room. The baby turned on its own. I ended up having an 8-pound-2-ounces bay girl and 19 and ¾ inches long. I named her Ayla. I already knew that if I had a girl someday, her name would be Ayla. Kevin cut the umbilical cord. He never had any children, so this was an experience that he would never forget. I couldn't believe my eyes. What a beautiful gift from God! I was so full of love and joy. This was by far the best day of my life! She was so beautiful! I loved her with all my heart and soul, like no love I had ever experienced before. I was so proud to be a mother. This was unbelievable, only a mother would know this feeling.

Thank you, God, for this precious baby. I am in love beyond what words can ever describe. I will cherish this child of mine forever and always. I feel so very blessed and am crying tears of joy.

Mom and Dale were so excited to see Ayla and everyone, of course, was surprised that I was holding a girl instead of a boy. I felt so happy and just wanted to hold my baby forever. They took Ayla to get her cleaned up and would bring her back to me when they were finished. I took a good look at her because I heard stories of babies being switched. I was going to make super sure that didn't happen! I was already being a protective mother and she was only a few minutes old. I knew that I would protect her for the rest of my life. I only wished to be a good mother. The doctor and specialist let me know that I was blessed for sure, but unfortunately, I would not be able to have any more children. It would be too dangerous, and they were thankful that everything turned out well. They said they could make sure I have no more children right away and take care of this. I explained that I would take care of it and not have any more children. I was thinking in my head that they told me this at 16 and look I have a baby girl. I didn't want them to know what I was thinking though. I kept my mouth shut and assured them that they didn't need to worry. When they brought Ayla back to me, a nurse asked for everyone to leave the room for a little bit. She taught me how to breast feed, and Ayla took to it right away. This was another experience that I felt overjoyed with. I felt so connected to Ayla and couldn't stop looking at her. She was truly everything I imagined plus more. I loved how she smelled and how close we already were. It's too bad that men don't get to go through this kind of connection because it is the best! I'm sure God knew what he was doing though and that they get blessed in other ways. My life just changed forever in many good ways. It was time for me to grow up and make sure this baby had the best mother I could be. I would put all my heart and soul in doing just that. I wanted to give her a good, healthy, happy life! She was my baby girl! I felt very comfortable being in the hospital. I think the nurses let me hold Ayla more than the other mothers for some reason. There were a few times I even fell asleep with her and normally that was not allowed. I just wanted her in my arms every breath I took. I even talked them into bringing her bed into my room with me. I always wanted her with me. They went against some rules for me and checked on us often. They told me that I was such a good mother. That made me feel good to hear that from the professionals. The night before I was to bring my sweet baby home, I'm not sure what happened. I could not stop crying and I wanted to just stay at the hospital. I didn't want to go home. I felt so comfortable and safe. A nurse talked to me and told me not to worry, she said, "You have the baby blues. This is normal and will pass soon." She explained to me about the hormone changes and that they call it the baby blues. It happens to all new mothers. I was surprised thinking my mom went through this too. It was hard to imagine. I usually could control myself from crying for no reason. This was weird. Thank goodness the next morning when I woke up, I wasn't feeling like that anymore. Thank goodness it only lasted a day and not longer. Lori came and picked us up and we went home. I hid in my bedroom for a few days. I studied Ayla so much, I knew every inch of her. I was very shy with breast feeding and chose not to do it around others.

My brothers wrote a letter to me and put it under my bedroom door. They said that they missed me and wanted to spend time with Ayla and me as well. They said Mom and Lori really wanted to spend time with us too. Could

Ayla and I please come out and watch a movie with them? I couldn't refuse that and thought I guess it was kind of rude of me to lock myself up with my baby and not let anyone in. I came out and they each took turns holding Ayla. My mother was in love big time! It was hard to have her give Ayla back to me. I was happy to see her so happy and the love she had in her eyes while studying Ayla. She kept giving Ayla kisses.

Ayla was such a good baby, but she really wanted mommy more than anyone else. When it was time to feed her, I would go back in the bedroom and do it. While I was feeding Ayla, I felt like someone was in the room. Suddenly, I smelt the smell of my father. Ayla suddenly looked up and stared. Then it was gone. I am not sure how to explain this to anyone, so I think I will let this be personal. I really did feel his presence though. I was not going crazy, I still had my mind. The baby blues were history! This was very real to me and I believe to Ayla too. She had her eyes closed and opened them and stared up like she was looking at me, but she wasn't looking at me and she even smiled. Some things are just truly amazing. I feel that Dad came and saw us. He is still the best dad ever!

He sure would have been a great grandpa. I could only imagine what he would have been like with Ayla. I'm sorry she didn't get the chance. She would have really loved him too. He was so special! I just really can't compare anyone to him. He was one of a kind! I feel at peace right now.

Everything was just perfect! I had been keeping in touch with my sister Elaine and my brother Orville through letters. I had been sending them pictures and to Bobby's parents. I felt it was the right thing to do. They were Ayla's grandparents and such wonderful people. I will always have a special love for them. Many people had been stopping over to see Ayla and bringing gifts. Even the guys that thought it would be a good idea to date.

They were all so kind to bring us such nice gifts. I felt over joyed by this. I decided that I better bring Ayla to Target so she could meet a bunch of special people. When I walked in, I could not believe all the attention we got. Target had more than gone out of their way for us. Even though they had a big banner saying Congratulations! It's a Boy! I laughed and said they needed to change that to girl! They showed me that I made it in the paper for going to labor at work. I laughed and thought that was funny too. When I saw my gifts that Target got for me, I could not believe my eyes. Everything I could imagine needing, even a crib. I cried tears because this meant so very much. I felt that these people cared so much. How did I get so lucky? This had to have been Godsent. I feel so thankful and happy. I let them know that I would be ready to come back to work soon. Many of them told me that I didn't look like I had had a baby. They said I looked great! That made me feel good. I was wearing my jeans again, but my shirts were bigger because of breast-feeding, I still had these enormous boobs. I didn't think much of boobs anymore. I couldn't get people to look at my eyes when talking to me, it was obvious where they were looking; it made me very uncomfortable. I wasn't used to this kind of attention. When I got home with my gifts, there was more company with gifts. Wow, the people were so kind. I really was well taken care of.

Before I could go back to work, I had to pump milk and figure out a bottle that Ayla would take to. The only one she would accept was the nuk. I didn't believe in using pacifiers, so I didn't have to worry about that. I knew that Mom never used pacifiers on us. I figured if you don't teach them a habit then they won't learn it or depend on it. It seemed like the right thing to do. I didn't want to train her to do something that I would eventually have to train her not to do. It seemed like foolish to me. It felt good to go back to work, but I missed Ayla terribly. If I didn't need to work, I wouldn't. I would rather be with Ayla. I was fortunate to have my mom there. At least I knew Ayla was well taken care of while I was at work.

As time went on, our lease was coming up and I was thinking of my sister and her children. I really felt the need to bring Ayla up around them. I also knew that Mom was going to want to get back to North Dakota soon. I thought about and prayed about it. It appeared my sister needed me too. I talked to Kevin and Dale and let them know what I was thinking. I let Lori know too. Kevin decided he would come with me. Lori and Dale wished to stay. Dale liked his job and they were getting along well. I wrote my sister and asked what she thought? She wrote back filled with excitement and said her daughters and husband were also excited. She said that it would be easy to get a place to live. Also, she assured me that I would be able to find a job easily too. I put in my two weeks' notice at Target. They were so sad and begged me to stay. I let them know that I couldn't handle the heat and needed to be around my family. They understood but still were sad to see me go. I would miss them too but knew that they would be fine without me. I had to think of the future of Ayla and myself. I felt it was very important to keep the family close. My youngest niece was close in age with Ayla. Jerilyn was her name. I thought it would be neat for the cousins to grow up together and play together. This was an important part of my younger years. I believe family is so important. My other two nieces Chynna and Krysta were very important to me too. I badly wanted to be able to spend good quality time with them and be their aunty. I was hoping to give them good memories that they could have forever. They were all so beautiful, I couldn't wait to see them. My sister was a good mother and now I was one as well. We had something in common that we could build on. I never got to know my sister closely because of her being deaf and gone a lot as I was growing up. Writing letters, we had connected in such a beautiful way and I loved her so much. I looked forward to spending more time with her. My brother Daryl could be an uncle for Ayla and I missed him so much! It would be so nice to be around him again. This felt like a very good choice and I felt so good about this. My sweet Ayla and I could go begin our life. I was so ready! Mom wouldn't have to fly back, she could ride with Kevin and me.

I was getting so close to Mom. I had been yearning this for years. She was my sidekick now and we got along so good. She always would tell me how proud she was of me. That was so special. I realized this was needed for her too. I wanted to carry this relationship forever and never lose it no matter what. I was proud of my brother Kevin and my brother Dale too. It sure was nice to be so close to each other. We had a lot of good laughs too. We all enjoyed laughing and being happy. Dale was good at making everyone laugh a lot. He was always up to something. Usually something funny.

It was getting close to leaving time to go to North Dakota. We were all packed and ready to go. I think we were all ready for this new change. It was hard to say goodbye to Lori and Dale. At least we could keep in touch. You never know with the winters in North Dakota, it would be nice to come see them. They could also come visit us too. That was the plan to do just that. Thank goodness for phones too. We hugged and said our goodbyes.

Chapter 16

Being a Single Mother in a Small Town

After a long travel, we finally arrived at my sister Elaine's house. It was so nice to be out of the vehicle and in a home. My nieces were so excited and happy. Everyone was so happy to see Ayla too. My sister's husband Randy was deaf too. He was the kindest man and such a good husband and father. Our family adored him. Elaine made everything comfortable for us, so we could get some sleep after our very long adventure. We were all exhausted. It was nice to be able to crawl into bed with my precious baby and go to sleep. When we woke up, I decided to go and see if I could find a place to live. Elaine told me about the apartments she used to live in had an opening and who to talk to. I arranged to see the manager and he had me fill out the paper work. He figured I would be able to move in very soon. He figured around two or three days. I was so excited! Things were working out already. I drove to Devils Lake and got signed up for the help I needed until I could find a job. Mom decided she would stay with me for a little bit. I really was thankful for that. Kevin would be staying with me temporarily until he could get a job and a place of his own.

I already knew this and was fine with it. We just had to take one day at a time and do the best we could each day. I knew that God would take care of us. He always does. He knows what is best for all of us all the time.

We just needed to have faith and trust him. It was also very important to me to get Ayla baptized as soon as possible. I also looked forward to going to church again. There were so many things that I needed to do that my mind was just racing. *OK, let's take each day and get us much done as possible. Make a list and check it off. I can do this! I just got to keep moving forward. Let God lead me!*

Sometimes it was hard for me to give things to God because I felt that I could take control. No matter what, God sent me back to him. It's just the way it was! Once I would do just that everything would go perfectly! *Trust God no matter what and he will take care of you.* This I kept finding out and it was like magic! God did take care of me and made everything possible and everything worked out perfectly. I got my home, church, Ayla baptized, and even got work. I even met some wonderful friends who I would cherish forever.

Eventually as time moved on and it was just Ayla and I, I found the love of my life. He was like an angel sent to me from God. I don't think I ever could have asked for a better man to become part of my life. He saw something in me and believed in me. When others were kicking me down, he was picking me up. He was very handsome too. I lucked out. We ended up living together for quite a few years and then one day he proposed to me and asked me to be his wife. At the time we were living in Montana and I was working a lot of hours to keep things good for us. We planned the wedding and invited friends and family. My brother Orville said he would give me away on this special day since I didn't have a father with me to. That meant so much to me. I looked forward to be a bride. His family treated me like I was a part of their family. I fell in love with all of them. I felt so blessed and thankful.

From that day forward, we decided to make our lives better and to start some business. We bought our own jobs and became partners. My downfall was that I started to have migraine headaches just as my mother did. While going through these headaches, I realized how much she suffered. I had to get away from noise and light. I would go home and lay down and hope the pain would just end. I would pray so much through these experiences. I didn't know that they had medicine for migraine headaches, so I would suffer for hours. I would cry and pray, that was all I could do. At the time I was studying to become Catholic. I was told about the Rosary and how powerful that prayer is. I kept trying to figure out how to do it and teach myself. I had no idea what I was doing. I think Mother Mary felt sorry for me and decided to help me. She helped me memorize the Sorrowful mysteries even though it wasn't the days for them to be said. She wanted me to start with learning them first. The sorrowful mysteries are about the suffering and pain Jesus went through until he was crucified. I found it interesting that I thought I was suffering but when I went and reflected on what Jesus went through, my suffering seemed so small. I was brought up Lutheran and for some reason I thought when people prayed the Rosary that they were sinning because we only have one God. After I learned it is reflecting on passes in the Bible and realized more about it,

I felt so foolish for thinking that way. It is a meditation on very important parts of the Bible. I also believed that only Catholics could pray the Rosary. That wasn't true neither. I am thankful that Blessed Mother Mary taught me the Rosary and helped my memory be able to do it without looking at a book. When suffering a migraine headache, you don't want to try and read. Even though I only memorized the sorrowful mysteries, there was a reason behind that too. By the time I would finish doing the Rosary, my migraine would go away. I couldn't believe how quick this worked. People were right, this was very powerful. *Wow, Mother Mary, you're fast!* I would do it more and more and watch my prayers be answered.

There are a lot of people that have known about the Rosaries I have done for them. It always fascinated me to see the prayers be answered. This everyone should do! This really works! I couldn't wait to get everyone doing this so that their lives could be so much better. I was so excited and so happy to let others know this! There wasn't Facebook at the time or I would have been blasting this one for sure. I wanted everyone to enjoy this wonderful experience that I was having. I would tell others and they for some reason would not take me seriously. I kept trying anyway and people responded much different then I was hoping. Fine I would start praying the Rosary and pray while doing the Rosary for them to start doing it. They won't know what hit them. Funny how their response made me do it more. I got so busy with this and forgot about myself. Before I could finally become Catholic and my daughter as well, we had to make a confession. I brought in my note pad to make sure that I didn't leave anything out. I wanted make sure to bring up all that I had done wrong in my life. My daughter Ayla and I went to the Church to do Confession.

She was a teenager at the time and boy did I wish I could be a mouse in the corner and listen to hers. She decided that she would go first. She was in there for 5 minutes and came out smiling. *What in the world is this! Good grief she needs to get her butt back in there! Seriously? 5 minutes? You're smiling? This isn't right!*

I couldn't say anything, but I am sure my face said enough. Now it was my turn. I was trembling inside. *How will the priest like me anymore after I get done doing this? This is much harder than asking Jesus to forgive me.* When you are sitting in front of a priest telling them all the bad things you have done, it really takes a lot of courage. I needed to do this! I hoped he would still like me when I finished.

After a box of Kleenex and who knows how long, I felt relieved. The priest was amazing and gave me so much good advice. He made me feel good instead of bad. It was like I really was in front of Jesus. All the heavy weight I had been carrying around was gone! I felt light and good and so relieved.

Ayla said, "Geez, Mom, that took a long time!"

I said, "You're a teenager. I had to go back a lot of years so I'm sorry, but I had a lot of years on you."

I decided to go to confession once a week and sometimes I would tell the priest that I remembered some other things that I forgot to bring up during my first Confession. During the week there would be a very old man and me. Nobody else would go to Confession. I was surprised that we were the only two sinners. One time, the priest told me that if I wanted anything else I could think of, I could just write a letter to God. He assured me though that my sins were already forgiven. When I went home, I thought about it and just in case I better cover my butt and write a letter to God too. After I finished with my letter to God, I put it in my Bible on my bed stand next to me. I knew this would be a safe spot since nobody else in my home cared to read the Bible but me. I felt much better inside. I felt I really connected with God and that he was with me. I knew he was listening to everything I wrote to him and could tell he was watching me cry about the moments I wished I could take back and do again. He understood. He is so loving and forgiving. My mind was finally at ease and at peace. I was so grateful that I did this, and it really helped me so much. Now I could try and be the person that God wished for me to be. I wanted to please him, not hurt him. I really wanted a second chance at life to be good in God's eyes. He had done so much for me, now I wished to do so much for him.

From this day and moving forward I will be whatever God wishes. Let his will be done. I trust you, Jesus, with all my heart and soul. I love you with all my heart and soul. I forgive all those who have done wrong to me and ask to be forgiven to all those I have done wrong to. Please make me a better person and help me to do what you need of me. I am ready! I got Jesus in my pocket and I am ready!

I forgot about my note because I felt so good now. I really felt like I was a changed person for the better. I was happy with myself and wished others could have this feeling I had. I was nothing without God, but everything with him. About a month had passed and I still felt so good until I happened to get a migraine again. I let my husband know what was going on and told him I better get home and lay down before it gets too bad. He said no problem and that he would take over doing what I was doing. When I got home, I laid down on my bed and began doing the Rosary. I fell asleep. I woke up because someone was in my room. I thought it was my husband but to my surprise it wasn't. I was startled at first.

I said, "Oh! It is you!"

I was relieved. I knew who it was immediately. It was blessed. Mother Mary. She was bent down beside me and reached in my Bible. She was grabbing my letter to God. Her face was so close to me. Her eyes were brown. She had the most innocent looking eyes I had ever seen. They were olive shaped and so beautiful. It was like I knew her all my life. I recognized her right away. There was no question about it. We made eye contact, but she didn't say anything. I could tell she was on a mission. I knew exactly what she was doing. She didn't have to speak, her eyes talked to me. Another thing that was happening was that the room smelled like roses and lilies. My room became like a flower shop but better. I recognized this smell, I talked about it previously. Now finally I could connect the smell.

It was her. She looked at me and smiled with my letter to God in her right hand. She let me know that she was bringing it to where it belonged. Not with words but with her eyes. She nodded at me. I had never seen eyes like hers before. They were so loving and pure. Her nose reminded me of my sister's nose. They were very similar. Her mouth was petite looking. Her smile was so sweet and loving. Her skin was olive toned and so flawless. Soft looking like a child. Her hands were small and graceful. She moved so flowy. She was wearing all white and it was flowy too.

When she left the room, she left so gracefully, looking down at me with my letter to God. Then she was gone. I felt so blessed at that time that I didn't even want to leave the room. I folded my hands and said Thank you! I felt like a ray of warm sunshine was in the room. My bedroom didn't even have windows and was always dark. Now it was full of warmth and light. The only feeling I had surrounding me was love. My heart and soul were floating with love, joy, and peace. This is so hard for me to put into words. The only way I can explain it is to take someone you love more than anything and multiply it times billions. I never ever wanted this feeling to leave. It was by far the best feeling I have ever experienced. If I could give everyone this, we would have a perfect world. All of us would just love! Love like we never loved before! This love was bigger than the sky. This love was bigger than the whole world! I will never be the same again! If this is how Heaven feels then I want to make sure I go there!

This couldn't get any better! This was the best day of my life! Nobody would ever want any more than this! It was really something! How could Satan deny this? What a fool! No wonder he is so angry! He made a mistake that ruined him forever and he can never have this again. He decided it so now he must pay the consequences of his decision. I really hope to all who read my story that you trust me and choose God! It will be a good choice and bring you peace love and joy. I can honestly promise you this! Please know that God is most definitely real! Heaven is real! Whatever you have done, don't worry, God will forgive you if you have a heart to heart talk with him. He loves you! He is just waiting for you to ask. If you do this, he can come into your life and bless you with many good things! Trust and believe in him! He really does love you! God loves us so much. God has plans for you! You are here for a reason. Let him in. Clean your plate with him and let him in, please. Even if we live to be 110 years old, life is so very short. Heaven is forever! Imagine not having any more worries, suffering, pain, and be in full happiness forever and ever! I want to see you in Heaven! My prayers are truly with you now, please join me and surrender! I have seen it, felt it and experienced it. This is so real. Please don't make the same mistake as Lucifer. God will provide and take care of you. We all have love in our hearts and it is time to let it shine! Don't let the world drag you down, stay above. Stay away from negativity and you will feed your spirit with joy. The biggest wish in my heart is for everyone to believe, feel, and see! It's the truth and that is why I chose to name this story TRUTH. People can all relate to a genie granting a wish. This is my wish for all of you to find what I have found. We can change the world!

Together let us unite and surround the world with love! Are you ready? I am ready too! Let's just do it! If this wish comes true then you will understand why I wish this! It doesn't matter what color or religion we are! We can all show love, be love, feel love, and do love! It's time! OK, let's do this! When Blessed Mother Mary came to my room, I knew that she is still working for us and trying to help us. She wants everyone to have and experience God's love! It's not about her, it is about what she knows. She just wants to bring everyone closer to her loving son Jesus!

She loves us so much as a mother that she wants us to have this. She is our helper! She always has been. God chose her, and she has a big job! I just love her to pieces! The times that you feel all alone, I get and understand because I have felt that too! In fact, many times. Now that I know the TRUTH, I never feel that way anymore. I never get scared any more. I just want you so badly to understand this. We all have our cross to carry but let Jesus help you and it will become lighter and pass. Adam and Eve screwed up and now we have free will. Stop running your thoughts and decisions. Let the one with the most power take over and trust him.

Let his will be done! Trust him because he knows what your purpose is. None of us have the power to move mountains but I know someone who does! Put on the armor of God and go be the best you can be! Let your light shine and get fired up because it will be a joyride! I am so excited about this! I just want to shout to the world and let everyone know! I have more energy! I enjoy life! I am truly so happy and full of joy! You can be like this and have this too! Come join me and let's rock this world with love! I am not done with you yet because as time passed, I became closer and closer to all the above. I have witnessed miracles through prayer. I have also seen and witnessed the most amazing things and have pictures of proof. The different experiences that I have struggled and used prayer with have helped me face my crosses that I have carried. In 2008, I was told that I have ovarian cancer. This was a real scare considering all the family members that I had lost to cancer. I felt my life was going to end. I trusted God that whatever his will was for me that I would obey. Although I really wanted to buy some more time if I was able to. It humbled me in so many ways. I was always one to care about my looks, my fashion, my car, and home. I was so busy making sure that I had all the important things until I realized my life was in jeopardy. The things that I thought were so important to impress others weren't anymore. The important matters became real to me. My husband, children, grandchildren, friends, and family. They became more of my focus than material things. I wanted to give them all the time I could, knowing that they may not have much of me anymore. It broke my heart to watch how different everyone treated me. Instead of loving me and having fun with me, and enjoying our time with each other, they were feeling sorry for me and acting very different. I knew that they were afraid and understood. I just didn't like this kind of attention and wanted to just be happy with them. They were so busy with trying to do everything they could think of to try and keep me alive. It was taking the time away that I wanted so badly to spend. I felt prompted to settle my mind and go and pray. My best prayer-spot was in nature, so I decided to go for a walk to the river by our house. It is a two-mile walk there and back. When I arrived at the river, I sat down and stared at the sky for a while just listening to the beautiful sounds of the birds.

I then said, "Dear Heavenly Father, I give myself to you fully. I give all of me to you. I believe in you. I trust you. I love you with all my heart and soul. Heavenly Father, please help me to be the person you wish for me to be, so that when I do die, I can spend eternal everlasting life in Heaven with all of you."

At the time we owned a restaurant, bar, casino, rafting business, and rock company. My hands were full. I had great employees so that helped a lot. My husband and I went to the doctor together and the doctor pretty much let me know that I should just go live my life because Ovarian Cancer is considered a silent killer. He explained to us in details why it is so hard to detect and by the time they do, it is already too late.

He described it like sand. That is why it is so hard to detect. The survival rate is not good. The doctor was someone we had got to know over the years very well and appreciated his honesty. When we left that day, we both were scared and wondering what next. I knew that I had to prepare myself to get into Heaven. My life changed in a matter of seconds. Reality was very depressing. I told my husband that we must accept this and prepare for what was going to come. He didn't want to talk or think about it.

"Gosh! Can't we just go fish hunting and have some fun?"

He looked at me and said, "What are you thinking? How can you think of hunting and fishing at a time like this?"

I didn't want to tell him all the other things I wanted to do. For instance, let's go climb mountains, zip lining, maybe I should take flying lessons, let's go ride some scary rides, let's drive my car as fast as we can and blast the music. My mind was racing with so many things that sounded so fun. I want to do so many things! I had a teenage daughter, maybe she would be up for my ideas. These sad faces were killing me! My husband's brother who had cancer before and some other people that I knew who found out they had cancer had went to see this guy who specialized in natural medicine. My husband's brother Denver talked to us and said we needed to go see him. What do you have to lose? We decided why not. We set it up and it was only about 90 miles from where we lived.

My husband couldn't get away from work so Denver said that he would go with me. We went, and I was very skeptical of this because I figured if there was a cure for cancer then everyone would already know this. I decided not to tell this guy what was going on to see if he could figure it out with this machine he had. I was testing him. After he got done getting my read out, he explained to me that I had ovarian cancer, but he could take care of it for me. Wow! This really was incredible. He put me on some natural herbs to take and told me to come back in two weeks. He said not to worry that he would get me feeling better. This was good news. I was overjoyed that God had sent this my way. I was also told to stay away from alcohol and sugar because cancer feeds into those. Obviously, it wasn't my time yet. God knows everything, and he put medicine for us to use if we just knew how. I was already feeling better and more comforted.

I was still going to confession once a week. I told my priest what was going on. He suggested we do a healing anointment on me. He said he had seen it work miracles. I never heard of it but said OK. I let my husband know everything that happened with the natural medicine guy and our priest. We, as a family, my husband, daughter, and I went to the priest after Mass and he did a healing anointment on me. After he was through and we left, I told my husband and daughter how hot his hands felt when he was touching me and praying over me. I could tell something miraculous happened. I just knew it! This was a good day! I felt at peace. My mind still wanted to do things though.

We should live life. We only get this life once. We should live it. Owning a bar and dealing with the public, sometimes people would annoy me. After all of this I wasn't annoyed anymore and saw good in everyone. I stopped joining in on gossip because I couldn't do that anymore. It made me feel bad. I didn't have to confess that anymore. I realized that I had been gossiped about many times in my life and how it made me feel. I surely didn't want to be a part of doing this to someone else. Why throw stones at people? There is good if we just take the time to overlook the bad. The good means more than the bad anyways. Of course, that would be different if it was bad as far as killing and raping… I'm just talking common errors people do. It's part of growing and changing, not of criticizing and condemning. Once again bring the love back. Going through this cross of mine made me a better person in many ways. I opened my heart and eyes and saw with love. This was something that I needed to change about myself. I felt so much better doing this. I started to appreciate little things that I use to overlook with my own selfish behavior.

I realized how many others have shown me love but I over looked it. I think I got educated more than a college degree at this point. What I was learning were a lot of things that made me feel better as a person and made me realize the things I needed to change about myself as a human being.

Life is too short to act so unkindly. Nobody should be treated like they're below me. Nobody is below me. I remember thinking that I was smarter than some people and learned later what a fool I was. I just didn't give them the time to show me how they were smarter than me in many things. I felt so terrible for being such a snob. What in the world was I doing? That is just so terrible. Shame on me! I will never do this to people again ever! I also realized how I had missed out on some great friendships from my own stupidity. Every one of us is the same, I don't care! We all have a reason for being here. Sometimes people can be grumpy and rude. Who cares! We don't know what they have been through and we all have our days. I used to be so rude that if someone treated me like that, I would confront them and let them have it! Now I smile and tell them I hope your day gets better. I also say a silent prayer for them. I could kick myself in the butt for some of my behavior! I don't ever want to hurt anyone ever again. I think about some of the guys that were so nice to me and wished to have a date. I was so rude to some of them and would tell them, "Can't you take a hint? Just leave me alone because I will never ever date you." Well, gee, that wasn't very nice of me.

None of them deserved that! I can't redo the past, but I sure can the present. I used to judge people so quickly. My goodness, who did I think I was. I think when it comes down to it and taking a good look at myself, I could really be a brat! God forgive me! Have mercy on me! I most definitely have no right to judge! Well the good news is that I took a reality check with myself. I went from being a brat to being loving and kind. I help homeless instead of throwing cans at them. That sounds bad, doesn't it? I would throw cans out my window thinking they could turn them in for money. I wasn't trying to hit them in the head. Sometimes I would on accident though. I admit it. Now I give them food or take them shopping for food even if they smell bad. People will look at me weird while I shop with a bum, but I just don't care. I got Jesus in my pocket and he is with me and sees the stairs. As far as I am concerned, I met a new friend. I just showed love. It's amazing how when you help someone out, it really feels so good. I usually don't even tell anyone I did it because it's between Jesus and me. Everyone has a story, that is for sure. We all do and that is the truth. I want my story to be good and filled with love.

How do you want yours to be? Something to think about. If someone tells me that I can't change the world, I tell them no I can't. We can though with Jesus. He is full of miracles and always has been. I am going to give it a try! What do I have to lose? I just need all your help! We can do this, I just know we can. The world needs this. It is time to show love and receive love back. Pray for the Holy Spirit to give you prompts and he will. He will also send you people that you need or maybe they need you. It is still all about love. We need love back. This world has got so full of hate and cruelty. We need to bring love and kindness back. God is full of love and we should be to. If we can get love back, I promise there will be nothing but good come out of it. If you're reading this, please say yes and help me. Earlier when I said I have been blessed with many blessings and seen with my own eyes true miracles, I have and want all of you to have this too. It isn't hard to do. Pray and get clean with God. Seek forgiveness with your heart and soul. Start your day with God and end your day with God. The rest will come! Remember to choose wisely what you feed your spirit. Keep negativity far away. Oh gee! A miracle had happened to my family and me. It was now 2010 and I was cancer free!

Imagine that? How this bliss is! This is the truth. I listened to my priest. I listened to my brother in law, and most importantly, I believed! I am healthy as can be and consider myself a walking talking joy of blessings! I love life! I respect life! I love people! I respect people! I love God and am not afraid to talk about it! I am much wiser and a much better person since this experience. Like I said earlier, we all have our crosses to carry, but how we choose to carry them is how we will get through them. Jesus will lighten the load! I wish I had known this earlier in life. My life could have been much better, but now that I know this, I just want to help others. If you do these things and live life this way, then the presence of Jesus will be in you and show through you. I don't see why we couldn't change the world and the view of others. If we put Jesus in our pocket, then we should be able to do anything and achieve to bring love amongst others. I truly believe this is possible and can be done. Each one of us can give and receive from others the same thing. It will keep going on and on until we have changed the world. It is time to start this now before the world gets out of control. This is a good thing and will bring love to all.

God wants this too. It's in the Bible how we are supposed to be. We need to love and forgive. We all need to follow God's commandments and act like Jesus showed and taught us to. I understand that some days are sad days. It is OK to have feelings. God made us have feelings. The important part of this is how we respond to our feelings. If we just try and be like Jesus and carry him in our pocket with every breath we make, I promise we will be better and help others be better as well. This seems like the right thing to do.

As time went on, more obstacles came and passed. One obstacle came and changed our lives as a flip of a light switch. Just when things were going so well, another problem arose. My husband's mother was unable to live by herself. Her son that was caring for her couldn't do it anymore because she decided this. His other brother tried, and he got too stressed and couldn't handle this. It became our turn now. The problem was that she lived in North Dakota and we lived in Montana. We sold our restaurant, bar, and casino. We stopped the rock business and kept the rafting business. We found out that my husband's mother's house had been flooding. This was not good. All the houses where she lived were flooding. I was not taught about the Saints yet but had heard about them. I asked God to help me figure out what Saint to ask for help with this house. That evening, I woke up in the middle of the night and was prompted to pray to Saint Christopher. I got up and googled Saint Christopher and read all about Him. He was the Saint to pray for help with this matter and a good Saint for many other things as well. I got very educated about Saint Christopher and went back to bed. I asked him to please help us with this matter that we were in great need. The next day while talking to my friend Bridget, she told me to have Denver, my brother-in-law, sprinkle Holy water around the house and try that. My husband and I let Denver know over the phone. He went to the Catholic Church near him and did just that. We were unable to come help him at this point. We had to take care of things with selling our business.

Sebastian's ex-wife and two of his children helped Denver out. That was sure nice of them to help in a time of great need. Denver was working so hard at trying to keep his mother's house from flooding. We at this point could only help by praying. We felt so bad not being able to help him with the labor involved. He was doing a fantastic job and keeping in touch with us daily.

I am an animal lover. My cat Misty had got badly injured by something. I found her under a trailer and I think she went there to die. She was in such terrible shape. She could not move and barely meow. I brought her into our home and started caring for her. Nobody thought she would live. Everyone thought I was wasting my time with her. They even thought that they should put her out of her misery. I loved her so much that I wouldn't let anyone touch her and continued caring for her. I took a syringe and was forcing water in her mouth. I bought some soft cat food and was giving that to her too. I prayed to God to please give me the Saint that could help me with this matter. Instantly Saint Francis came to my mind. I googled Saint Francis and researched him. He was the Saint that could help me. I prayed that Saint Francis would please help me with Misty and to please let her live. After about a week, she was all better and doing very good. She was eating and drinking by herself.

She was still moving slow, but I was so thankful that she had improved and was better. *Thank you so much Saint Francis for helping me out.* When I educated myself about Saint Francis, I was amazed about a story of a wolf and him. I was thankful to learn about him because he was such an amazing man and now, I understood why he was a saint. I was also so thankful that God was literally letting me know the saint names for which I needed. I honestly didn't know a thing about the Saints but understood that they can help us. Seeing how they do made me realize what great helpers they are. My mother-in-law's house was the only house that didn't flood other than one other. The house beside her flooded too. I wonder what her neighbors thought. I must chuckle because it was so amazing.

This also helped Denver go back to church again and spend more time at the church in God's presence. This made him a believer. Thank goodness, because he had lost faith until this happened. He was so full of joy and peace. This helped him mentally, physically, spiritually, and in many other forms and ways. He was blessed and so were we. My mother-in-law, Eleanor was so very thankful too. We ended up getting everything done with selling our business. Now we had to try and sell Eleanor's house, so she could move in with us. This was not a good time to do this being as her neighborhood was a flooded mess. I let my priest know what was going on and he advised us to get the Saint Joseph statue on selling the house and follow the instructions. We found one at a Christian store and bought it. We than followed the instructions in the packet and did exactly what they said to do. We said a prayer that this home would go to whomever God felt needed it the most and would appreciate it and love it.

A week later the Real Estate Company called us and said the home had sold 164 for the asking price we wished for. Wow! That was fast! Eleanor got more than she had originally paid for it. We went higher thinking they would want to negotiate, but they didn't. This was so amazing!

Thank you, Saint Joseph, you are so amazing! Thank you so much! Thank you most Heavenly Father! We are so grateful! This is so miraculous! We figured it would take a long time for this to happen. All I can say is Wow! Now we had to pack and get ready for the big move! Eleanor was very excited. My husband's kids came and helped us a lot and Eleanor gave some stuff to them that would help them out too. She had very nice things. She and her previous husband used to own a bank. All her things were top of the line and beautiful. This was working out well and helping others as well. Soon we achieved getting everything done and we were on the road to Montana. With all the stops we ended up taking longer than normal. We left early in the morning around 5am and arrived at our home around 9pm. It was a good drive and I read some of the bible on the way home. I would talk to Eleanor and Butch about some of the things that I was reading. When we got home and got Eleanor to her bedroom, she loved it. Our animals were so happy to see us and Eleanor whom I call Ma was excited to bring her kitty that we named Bear. She had a choice between a grey one or a black one, so she chose the black one. Butch's ex-wife decided that she would like to have the grey one, so we gave her that one. Ma was wheelchair impaired at the time, so we built a ramp going into our home and made her bedroom wheelchair friendly. After some time had passed, we also added on to our home to make it more comfortable living for all of us. It helped a lot. She was pleased with all the company we got. Our friends fell in love with her as well. It was nice for our relatives to be able to stay with us and be able to spend time with all of us at one time. Ma enjoyed crocheting, so we let her make hats for all her grandchildren and some of her great grandchildren as well. Her and I were making dishcloths too. It was very fun. We added some of her things from her house to our home, so she would feel like it was her house too. We wanted her to know that this was her home too. She enjoyed having her hair and nails done once a month. I would spend the day with her letting her be pampered. She loved to shop so when we were in Missoula, I would take her shopping for clothes. She always thought she was smaller than what the clothes said and thought her feet were two sizes smaller than what they were. This made a long and interesting day for us and the women helping us. I usually wasn't a very patient person and really wasn't a shopper unless it was a good second-hand store, so this was a real test for me. The more time I spent with her, it didn't take long for me to realize that she liked a lot of attention and liked to spend a lot of money on herself. We were quite opposite that way, but we had other things in common. We both loved being in the kitchen and cooking and canning. There were some things that bothered me about her being so self-centered, but I had to accept her for who she was. We got her an excellent doctor who changed quite a bit of her medications. We also got her into physical therapy three times a week. She was doing the swimming pool therapy. Her back issues and arthritis issues were challenging because she was always in such pain. After many doctor appointments we also realized that she had zero tolerance for pain. The doctor decided to try epidermal shots and see if that would help calm down some of her pain issues because she was using only pain pills and Tylenol for that. The Tylenol never seemed to work but the pain pills did help. After months of doctoring and physical therapy, we were finally able to get her out of a wheelchair and walking again with a cane. This was good. She still had lower back pain issues but was really doing fantastic. She had a temper on her and would like to yell. I really tried avoiding this because I would rather have peace. Somehow though she would bring out my temper and I would get stressed out. It took a long time to get used to this behavior and adapt to it. I would find myself apologizing just to have peace. Deep down inside I felt like I was apologizing when she should have been doing this instead. I learned that I had to do this, or it would never end. When Denver would come visit, they would fight. She would fight with my husband. It was getting ridiculous so of course I turned to prayer after venting to my daughter or close friends first. I just wanted everyone to be happy. We should all be thankful and happy. Our lives are good and getting better every day. This added drama was not even necessary. Her sister Mary would come stay with us and that would be such a relief. Her sister was the kindest woman and so thankful for everything. It was so pleasant to have that breath of fresh air in our home but after a week, she and Ma would be in a battle too. Her sister told me, "I don't know how you can do this because she is a handful. One of my friends said she doesn't care if she gets bad attention or good if she is getting attention. She told me that when she is trying to stir up trouble, you just must ignore it and not feed into it." She said ignore the bad and feed the good. That was the best advice I had gotten from anyone. God had to really work with me on this though because it was hard to do. It was easy to say but so hard to do. Ma knew all the right buttons to push with the people that loved her. She would be deceitful sometimes and act like something medically was wrong to get attention too. We would bring her in and after checking everything they could check and find out nothing was wrong, then she would be happy and smiling all the way home. This became a habit and we had to keep bringing her in because how would we know if it was true or for attention if we didn't. It was like the cry wolf story. Bottom line was when I would ignore the bad and feed the good, we would end up spending the day at the hospital to find out nothing was wrong. I had never dealt with a personality like this before, so this was shocking to me that people were even capable of doing this. She was a very smart woman but used her intelligence in fooling with our minds. This was very hard on me, so I had to turn to God. I prayed so much for God to help my husband and me out because this was too hard on us. If we had her surrounded by people and she was getting all the attention, she was fine. If we had her shopping and getting her hair or nails done, she was also fine.

The problems arose when this was not happening or if I was getting attention instead of her. She really hated that. She would find a way to pull the attention from me and put it towards her no matter how she had to do that. When around others she would turn into a totally different human being and be so sweet and loving. She would even tell everyone how much she loved me. If I would tell a friend how she would act with us, they looked confused because they couldn't imagine her being this way. IF someone would come stay with us long enough, they would see it for themselves. I didn't have to tell them. It was a great surprise to many. If we would hire one of our friends to stay with her when needed, she would see how she could be too. It wasn't just when we were around. It really was all about attention. My confessions were repeated that I got mad at my mother-in-law again. My husband was going to confession for the same reason. One time the priest wanted to know where she was and if she was coming to confession. I said, "No, she doesn't think she has anything to confess." Oh, dear God the look on his face was priceless. After time had went on and the doctor seen her numerous times for absolutely no reason medically found and it being attention, he decided that she needed to be psychotically examined. He lined up the appointments for this to happen. After two days of being mentally examined, they found out that she had ADHD and a compulsive disorder. They found out many other things that they couldn't share with me but were very concerned about my welfare. They had three huge books that they wanted me to read to help with coping with this type of behavior. They talked to me about these things in front of her. She didn't like hearing what they were saying about her. They also let me know that she was extremely jealous of me. They said that caring for her was going to be very difficult on me and my husband because of her mental behavior. Everything they were telling me I already knew, so, in my head I really didn't need to read these thick books because I had already been through it and learned how to cope with it and so had my husband. Of course, later I wished I had read the books. Even though it had been a lot more work than we ever thought it would be and much more difficult to deal with, the mental mind games. Good also comes out of bad. I found myself reaching out spiritually and in positive ways to help me to deal with Ma. I knew that she wasn't going to change so I would have to but the only way I could was with God. I went on some retreats. I read more and more of the Bible. I was doing the Rosary and the seven sorrows every day, plus two hours of prayer and meditation daily. Through doing this I was becoming a better person every day. I was also feeling so close and connected with God, our most loving Father, and let Jesus live in me. The Holy Spirit stayed in my presence and would whisper in my ear or give me prompts. The blessed Mother Mary was coming to see me more often and kept visiting me. She and I would pray together.

She made me feel confident and joyous again. By her love for me and her help, I got undepressed and got revived. I realized the things that Ma would aggravate me with didn't anymore. When she was doing her deceitful things, I would pray for her rather than fight with her. I would show her love and just be kind and smile without faking a smile. I smiled because she reminded me of a child with bad behavior. Sometimes I would have to walk away from her and laugh because it was that goofy. Blessed Mother Mary taught me that even through bad we can make good out of it with love. If we just show love instead of anger, there will be no fight. It ends it. This became easier and easier as the days went on. I felt like I should thank Ma because if she hadn't come into my life, I would still be the same person and the changes I had made were changes that God was pleased with and so was I. I believed that by being willing to let my guard down and let God in to mold me the way he wished for me to be has helped find great happiness and peace with myself. If I have them, I can get through any cross that I need to carry, and it becomes much lighter than trying to carry it myself. Thank you, Ma. Forever I will thank you because without you I wouldn't have been desperate to make these changes. I have such a connection that I feel I can conquer the word! My strength is huge, and my love is even bigger! For a while, I spent days crying and my feelings were hurt. My self-esteem went down the tubes after being called horrible names by Ma. It battered my spirit and I became so depressed. I searched in the right direction for help and was so humbled that I found the light! I found life again! The power of prayer is so amazing, and God's timing is so perfect. Life can be hard if we try to take it on ourselves and it can even feel impossible, but the good news is we don't have to. Once we let God in and take over, life is much better. I am nothing without God but am everything with him. He is real and wants to help us so badly, but we need to ask. I look at life with clear eyes again just as I did as a child after being baptized. I recognize Satan and how he works when I didn't use to. I send him away and God does too. Life is as good as we make it or as bad as we make it but with God's love and mercy it is wonderful no matter what occurs. It's OK. I'm so thankful that I found this again because it sure is worth it! I still have the same life, I just deal with it from help from above. Satan loves it when we are weak, that gives him power to make us weaker and he will if you let him. You don't need to though and God always has more power than evil. Satan will try so hard to keep us from loving ourselves and loving God. He really can't win at this if we recognize it. What I have found is any time things are negative, nerve wracking, or destructive, to just look up and say, "By the power of God, leave now Satan. You are not welcome!" I, being Catholic, always do the Saint Michael Prayer as well. It works fabulously! I have even done this prayer in front of people when I recognize what is happening to them silently. It's amazing how they and even their face and body language changes within five minutes after doing this. They become at peace instead of in misery. Try it sometime and you will see results, I promise you this. I have even done it with badly behaved children and they usually change instantly. I did it with a three-year-old child. One time this child was out of control and I said it out loud. The three-year-old child thanked me and was full of peace. How did she even know what I did or what God did? Somehow the three-year-old knew to thank me and gave me a hug.

We need to be so carful in today's world on what we allow ourselves to listen to. The TV or music. It's all our free will. We need to be careful of what we choose to feed our spirits with. If it isn't love, it's best to avoid it. The news can be crushing for our spirits. The media can feed into negativity so much. I watch the news once a week instead of daily and I'm truly not missing anything by doing so. I choose music that makes me feel happy and like singing or dancing! There are all kinds of music to listen to. It doesn't have to be religious, just something joyful! I watch movies that make me laugh and smile, not get angry or terrified. Being in nature is so good for the soul.

Being in nature is my true favorite, but whatever you find for yours should make you feel good and happy. Sometimes just being in the kitchen is my happy spot, being as I love to cook and bake. Sometimes camping or fishing is my happy place. Sometimes hunting and being out in the nature providing food for our table and family is my happy spot. Sometimes just relaxing and reading an uplifting book is all I need. Sometimes I just go on a hike with my dog and get to the top of a mountain is all I need to embrace me with joy and peace. To be on top of the mountain and look down at the beauty God created makes my day! I even get a joy out of cleaning and organizing. Sometimes I just love playing with my pets and my chickens. There is just so many, I could go on and on. We all have talents God gave us and we all have different things that make us happy. Do these things and fuel your body and mind and spirit and soul! You will feel good about yourself and your spirit will feel so good too. I also feel so good when I help others. This is amazing how much I get out of doing and taking the time to help other people. I think God really likes it too. It seems when you give, you also get back. My dad used to always say what you put into life is what you will get out of life. Those words of wisdom have stayed with me since I was a young child. He was always happy and joyous until he got sick with cancer but even when very sick, he stayed positive and kept his smile.

Make every day great and make every day count so when you go to bed at night, you will sleep well knowing that you did just that. Don't let life get you down, let it build you up! Be the person you were born to be and always love who you are! God made you and God never makes mistakes! You are here, and you are great, let others see your inner beauty come alive! Enjoy your journey while you're here, none of us are here too long. Even if you live to be 100, life is still so very short. Let others enjoy your presence. Let them see your greatness! Let God help you discover yourself and shine your light for others! It's OK to love yourself! That is not being selfish! God loves you, so you should love yourself too! It doesn't matter who you are now. It does matter who you are tomorrow! Live life and don't let life live you! As time went on, we went through ups, downs, and true miracles. Ma became more work and harder to take care of. My husband and I had our ups and downs too but hung in there. I have learned that everything passes. It's no need to stress out because it shall pass too.

Chapter 17

Our Mother of Love!

I decided that I needed to have a refreshment of fueling my spirit up. I went on a retreat with a good friend of mine and brought Ma with to stay with her granddaughter. This would be a good getaway for all of us. Since I had just had brand new tires put on, I decided to drive. I liked driving anyway and would rather drive than ride. My dear friend Bridget who I call Angel most of the time because she is an angel to me, Ma, and I were all set and ready for our trip. Bridget and I would be staying in a motel together enjoying our retreat and some girl time. Ma would be staying with her granddaughter, husband, and their children. They are beautiful people with a beautiful family. We love all of them so much. Ma would be in great hands, so Angel and I could enjoy our retreat. We had about a five-hour drive to get to where we needed to be. While driving, we were having such good conversation that time seemed to pass quickly. When we almost arrived not too far away, the vehicle was acting so terribly. I couldn't continue driving like this, so I pulled over to figure out what was going on. Something seemed wrong with one of my tires. As I got out and looked, they seemed fine. I called my husband and explained to him what was happening. He let me know what to do and how to check everything on the tires. He had just brought it in to the mechanic and had tires put on, so this was odd. One of the tires didn't have the bolts tightened. He told me to use my fingers and tighten them as much as I could and then call a tire place for help. He was so upset that the mechanic didn't tighten these bolts. It apparently could have been very dangerous, and we are so lucky we didn't get in an accident driving the speed we were driving. My Norwegian blood comes out of me and says *ofuda*. Any time I do something that will lift my spirit with being closer to God our loving Father, things happen to try and keep me from making it. Funny how that works. We know who is trying to keep me from getting to learn more and feel more closer to our loving Christ, don't we? It happens every time, but God and I always win. It's just a temporary setback. Angel, Ma, and I felt so very thankful that we didn't have something terrible happen and that we were all safe. Who do you suppose oversees this good that could have been so bad, even fatal? We all recognized this and knew right away that this wasn't luck. My husband knew too and said, "Boy! God stepped in and took care of ya." Knowing this we felt blessed and good about things. After the tire place fixed our vehicle so that we could be safe, we began our adventure once again. My husband was going to deal with the mechanic back home, he was so upset with him. Angel, Ma, and I stopped at Ma's granddaughter's house first. We stayed and visited for a little bit. It is always so nice to see relatives that you haven't seen for a while. This was my husband's niece and her family. She felt like my blood niece though. Her children were such gifts from God and so was she. Her husband was the most pleasant man and truly was such a good husband and father. They really had a beautiful family. I enjoyed the visit so much but now it was time for Angel and me to find our motel and get checked in. After doing what we needed to do, we went shopping for a few things since we had time. It's always fun to shop for the grandchildren. Angel was on a mission and it was so fun. We went back to the motel to refresh and get ready for the retreat.

Angel and I were so excited for this!

Chapter 18

The Retreat That Changed My Views

A beginning of my spiritual life with Jesus. His Mother Mary, God, our precious Father, and the Holy Spirit. As a very young child feeling closely connected to Jesus. My Best friend, Jesus.

Now, I was brought back to understanding and loving him and Blessed Mother Mary beyond what I could have ever imagined. At this retreat I heard a story about what the woman had gone through during the genocide and how prayer saved her life and others. Forgiving those who had violently murdered, raped, and tortured. Forgiving those who murdered her loved ones and family. This opened my eyes to many things that I also needed to do to be good with God. She taught us the seven sorrows prayer from our loving Mother Blessed Mary. I realized as well that we needed to forgive in order to be forgiven for our own sins. Why should we let those who have hurt and damage us to take us away from Heaven? *I wish to go to Heaven and will do whatever it takes to get there. I must forgive so many and clean my plate.* I went to Confession and once again confessed my hardened heart to please forgive me and those who have hurt me so much through my life even as a young child. These people I ask for me to forgive and God to forgive as well. After Confession, I felt like a bundle of bricks were lifted off my chest and I had peace and love only in my heart. I surrendered my life, my heart, my soul to God and put all my trust in his will. I felt so good and so clean and pure again. This brought joy, peace, and love to my spirit and soul. Now I could begin my life with Jesus once again! My plate was clean and refreshed and I felt so very blessed. I thanked God for showing me the way to pure happiness! The seven sorrows were a prayer that affected me so much and brought me so very close to Blessed Mother that I was so excited to spread this news! Bridget, my sweet precious angel, felt the same! The woman at the retreat who had written a book and told her story was such a gift from God to help all of us! This made me inspired to help people as well.

We couldn't wait to get back home and spread the news! The woman told us that we shouldn't use the seven sorrows prayer to replace the Rosary but add it to our Tuesday and Friday prayers. I did it daily because it meant so much to me personally. I would tear up while doing it because of the pain and suffering that our precious Mother Mary went through. As a Mother I could relate and felt her pain and the pain of Jesus too. This brought so many tears to me. It was good for me to understand this and helped me feel so much closer to Jesus too! Bridget and I were so full of the Holy Spirit and so happy that we did this! After it was over, the woman was doing book signings. I ended up taking a walk with her as she held my hand. I felt like Jesus was holding my other hand as we walked and talked. I talked to her about

Blessed Mother Mary appearing to me and told her the story. I told her that I was afraid to talk about it because I didn't want people to think I was crazy. She let me know how I had been blessed! She said that I should be shouting with joy! She informed me that she travels to the places Mary appears just hoping this will happen to her. She told me to write another letter to God and see if she comes again. Her face was so full of joy for me. It was so pleasant, and she wanted my phone number because she wanted to visit with me more but didn't have time. We took a picture together and I gave her a book of mine that I had written and published called *This Happened* and used a pen name at the time, Faith Reise.

Here is a picture of us with my book on the table

I have prayed for her every day since then and still do because she truly captured my heart! She never did get back in touch with me but that is OK, I still love her dearly. I will always treasure my experience with her. Bridget and I went back to the motel and got our things packed and ready to go. We picked up Ma and met the relatives for something to eat. We had a wonderful visit and it was time to return home. The weather changed and turned very stormy. Everyone was so worried about our long travel home. I let everyone know that we will be fine. God will take care of us. Before we left to go home while in the car, I prayed for the weather to change and get us home safely. Instantly the weather changed, and the sun came out! We were all surprised and so full of joy and amazement of the power of prayer.

Even though it was a long travel, time went by so quickly and soon we were home. I dropped Bridget off at her house and then Ma and I went home. I missed my husband so much and was so happy to see him! I told him about our experience and wanted to share the sorrowful mysteries with everyone I could and so did Bridget. We were like a breath of fresh air and elaborated with the presence of the Holy Spirit on fire in us! When we went to church, we visited with many and were so excited to share our experience with others. One of my dearest friends Joe Rogers whom I absolutely adored was stricken with our encouragement and happiness. He asked that we do a special talk about our experience at his house with our

Church Journey team. We of course said yes, we will. Bridget and I were so excited and felt prayers answered to be able to do this. I made several copies of the prayer of the Rosary of the seven sorrows so we could teach all to do this and do it with them.

It was a wonderful night for all of us and the prayer was amazing. I think it affected everyone who was there. Now they could do it.

Here is a picture of the seven sorrows prayer that I took

This was a special night and we all felt so blessed. In the next few weeks I shared with many how powerful this prayer is and handed out the prayer books to all that I could. My daughter Ayla and I spent much time doing it together as well. This meant so much. We would take turns reading the prayers and it was time well spent. I have a statue of Blessed Mother Mary in my home. It is The Lady of Grace It is in the living room where I made a Shrine.

Here is a picture of the Statue of the Lady of Grace

Here is a picture of my shrine

Here is a front view of my shrine

One night I was troubled and praying the seven sorrows. I happened to look up at the statue and she became alive! She was big and flowing! Her arms were motioning me to come to her. I did just that! When I got to her, I fell to my knees.

She is so beautiful and so full of love and grace! She was so Heavenly and holy that I couldn't move. She was telling me so many things and letting me know that she was here with me!

She kept telling me, "I love you. You are my child! I weep with you! Every pain you feel I feel as well! I am here, sweet child! I will help you! Trust in me and I will bring you to my son!"

I could not speak! I was overwhelmed with love! My voice could barely speak but I thanked her and cried tears of love! I welcomed her in my life and home and asked her to please stay with me and never leave! I let her know how much I loved her and that I would do anything, just please don't leave!

She smiled and said softly, "My child, I will never leave you and I have been with you and always will remain with you, just trust and believe. I love you, Linda, now and forever! I love all my children and want to help all of them! I am just waiting for them to come to me! Vanish your worries! Your prayers have been answered and whomever seeks me will also seek my son! I always bring those to my son. Do not be afraid, I am well pleased! Continue bringing others to me!" She gave me a hug and kissed my forehead. She smiled the most loving smile I have ever encountered.

She went back to being a statue. I was so excited I couldn't wait to tell my husband! This was so wonderful, I really felt like jumping up and down and was so full of love and happiness! My mind felt so at peace! Wow! That's all that I could think! Wow! I was so thankful and full of glee!

Now I can conquer anything! I have Mother helping me! She is with me! I didn't expect this to happen again. I just treasured that it did! I know she is real! She came to me! She is so real! Wow! Why me? Oh well! I am just so thankful! I wanted everyone to know that she really is real! She really loves us! She really is our Mother! Her beauty and grace is incredible! Her love is so pure! My goodness! This was the best night of my entire life! Thank you! Thank you!

Thank you! I kept blowing her kisses! *I will treasure this forever and ever that is for sure! Our sweet Mother!*

Everyone needs to know and love her! This is so wonderful! She is there for us! She can help all of us! I still to this day will always be glorified for this night! I shall always have her as my mother and choose her to help me completely with this life! I praise her! Even though I thought that this was a once in a life time experience, she kept coming alive for me usually around 10 p.m. Got so used to her visits with me and her presence, but I knew not to expect it to keep happening. I was so grateful though that she would appear so much! I would talk about it with close family members and a couple of friends. I didn't publicize this because I felt it was personal. My friend Joe Rogers became very sick with cancer and was dying. When I went to see him in the hospital, I didn't realize that it would be my last time to see him. I had a Rosary tangled up with a scapular that I would hold at night when I would fall asleep. I had been doing this for years, so it was very worn out but so special to me. It was my comfort piece as I would sleep. Every morning it would still be in my hand. The Rosary was purple and the scapular brown. I spent so much time holding it and sleeping with it that it turned into a ball.

Here is a picture of it

While sitting next to Joe, I took it out of my pocket and talked to him about it. He smiled and asked if he could hold it. I let him. He said, "Linda, she sure loves you!"

I told him, "Joe, she really loves you too!"

He looked at me and said, "No, Linda, she really loves you!"

We prayed together, and I blessed him with holy water. We had some laughs too! When I was in Joe's presence, I felt like my dad was there. Something about him reminded me of my father. I loved being around him. It was time for me to leave and I asked him if he would like to keep the ball of love.

He said, "No, it's yours but thank you for letting me hold it! I got what I needed from it." I gave him a hug and kiss on the cheek and said goodbye.

The next day we got the phone call that Joe had passed. Even though I would miss him so much I knew that he was in good hands. He was also close to Mother Mary and had a shrine in his home. He also prayed so faithfully and did the Rosary and the seven sorrows. I knew he was going to be in Heaven and we would meet again. I will always feel blessed to have such a special friend and he will always be a huge part of my heart! His wife gave me two candles that he bought in Mexico of the blessed Mother and to this day they are on my shrine. They are the Lady of Guadalupe. If you look at the shrine picture you will see them. I think of Joe every day and pray a Rosary for him every day as well. I always tell people once you become my friend, I will pray for you daily until I die. I don't just speak words. I put my words into action. Thank you, Joe, for our beautiful friendship and being my brother in Christ. I have been blessed by having you in my life! I love you.

Joe Rogers had a brother named Jim. Jim was gone a lot, working. When he was home, he helped our church in so many ways. Joe and Jim were very close. Jim is also a very special friend to my husband and me. We would also try and help Joe's wife out when I could by giving her rides when needed. She had many others that helped her, so I wasn't needed much. She was a very sweet lady.

Our church is a small parish, but our hearts are big! As time continued our sweet Blessed Mother Mary would keep showing up. I became so friendly with her just like I was with my earthly Mother that I would show her things I would do. When I would bake homemade buns, I would bring them to her and show her. I love decorating cakes and cookies, so I would show her when finished. Most of the time I would get a nod and a smile. Sometimes she would remain a statue, but I knew she was watching everything I was doing. When troubled I would go talk to her as though I was talking to my earthly mother. Soon I would be at peace and soon after that my troubles would be fixed. If I would go to bed without saying goodnight to her, my own heart would be troubled. It would bother me so much that I would get back up and say good night. We would usually do the Our Father Prayer together at night. To this very day we still do. Even though I still miss my mom so much I feel that I have gained another. I miss my father too, but I have a Heavenly Father that most people relate to as God. I always call him Father.

If I can just take the time I have on Earth and make sure to do things so I can get to Heaven then I will see all the ones I have lost in this life and spend eternity in happiness! That is my goal! I choose this goal as my main priority if I am alive.

Chapter 19

Blessings After Blessings

As time passed, not only did I go through some very troubled times, but blessed Mother Mary was right. She helped me through, and I also became so deeply connected to Jesus through her intervention and help. I also feel so close to our most loving Father and I feel so loved! The Holy Spirit lives inside me each day. I feel honored! The trick to this is to never fall out of prayer. No matter what, keep the prayer. As prayers became answered right before my eyes, I always acknowledge this and say thank you. Praise God! Just as any parent they love it when we listen and say Thank You! When we pray, we must trust and believe! If it is not in God's will, our sweet Mother can intercede. If that doesn't work, then it's because God has something better in his will for us. We just need to trust this.

It took me so many years to learn this method and the realness of it. Now I feel so complete and happy that I have found the truth. I think of what Jesus and Mary went through. They were without sin and still suffered so much. They trusted God and knew this shall too pass. They knew to trust God and believe. They accomplished God's will and did it well. They gave us an example of how we should act and be. The world would surely be so much more pleasant if we all did just this. The hardest part of this is fully trusting. It is in our nature from growing and maturing that we lose trust. As a child we trust but as an adult we don't. To get that back I feel you must let go of all that have shown you not to trust and forgive. By forgiveness we really open the door for God our most precious Father to come into our spirit and soul. It is so hard to truly forgive those who have done so much damage to our being. It was one of the hardest things for me to forgive Tom and let that go. I had so much resentment for him and what he took away from me as a human being. Once I did forgive him, my spirit was lifted and relieved. It felt so much better than carrying all the ugliness that was taken over my thoughts and what was inside me that I had been carrying around for years. This felt so good for that to be relieved. The hurt and pain is gone and now I am so full of love. Confession was a big part of letting go of the hangers in my closet that were disturbing my sleep.

Once I got rid of all this negativity there was a huge change in me. The peace that was brought upon my spirit and soul was worth every bit of it. Yes, you can confess to God personally and he will forgive, but you also must remember once you do that your sins are forgiven. Don't carry that baggage any more. It's done now and let it go. Because of being Catholic we go to a priest for confession. Nobody must do it this way, we all can go straight to God. What I learned from going to confession after talking to priests about it was that they are working for God. They usually don't even remember what people confess because the Holy Spirit becomes alive in them. It truly is like sitting in front of Jesus and makes it much more personal and from the heart. The tissues are used in confession because of the real presence of our Lord. When doing this compared to going right to God, I feel the presence and it is more meaningful. It's hard to sit in front of a priest and ask for forgiveness of all the horrible things you have done, but reality is that is the Lord's presence and love that wraps you with peace. When I was Lutheran and confessed to God, it was fine, but this is very powerful. It's a personal choice and we are all God's children, so it doesn't matter how you choose to do it. The important fact is to do it! Once you do this, get ready because your life will become so much better! Now God can give you his Grace and be with you, live inside you, and you will be so grateful to have this. It is so much better. It doesn't matter what you have done, God's mercy and forgiveness is there waiting. It is also important to keep feeding your spirit. Read inspirational books and be careful what you choose to watch on TV. Don't damage what you have started. I have Jesus by my side in everything I do and if Jesus wouldn't watch it or listen to it then neither shall I.

I made a prayer-spot down by the river that I go to each day. I do prayers and a Rosary every single day. It is the only way to start my day. After taking the time to do this, my day is always great! No matter what crosses I carry I surrender to God's will and am not alone. They are with me through everything. The blessings I receive are outstanding and that is living! People think they don't have time and I used to think this too. We must make time. I get up earlier and it works out well. I figured out as well that time management is priority in our daily lives. Once you figure out how to manage your time, the stress lifts. It is worth it, and I have had moments where I wake up late and feel so crushed. I figure it out though and maybe I must do my prayers while driving instead of the river. I just know and have learned that if I choose not to start my day this way, my day will not go the way I would rather have it go.

Here is a picture of my prayer-spot at the river

As I go to the River and do my prayers and rosary, the sky talks to me in many forms and ways. Here are some examples but I could make a book just on pictures, being as I have so many of them.

Angel in the sky appeared while praying the angel prayer:

When Blessed Mother Mary appears:

This is a picture when driving and doing a Rosary, the
sky went from blue to rainbow colors on my 3rd mystery

Back at the River the sky went from normal to this unique blue
The colors in the sky change and dance for me:

When I asked in prayer to surrender myself to Jesus, a
cross appeared

Blessed Mother Mary appearing on the Mountain:

Things I did with rocks at my prayer-spot:

On the way to my prayer-spot while in prayer, the sky changes from gray to colorful rays of red, pink, blue, yellow, white, and purple.

When I get to the river to my prayer-spot

In my first chapter, when I wrote that I wanted to just remember one thing, even though I couldn't remember what it was, I feel God helped me to figure it out. I believe in my heart that I needed to remember to just trust God through this journey and let his will be done. I feel so complete now and at true peace. Mary and Jesus put all their faith and trust in him no matter what their challenges and trials were. They were a living example of that. Now that I have got this, and it took me long enough, I will always surrender to God's will with me and keep my faith. Most of all I trust him with everything and it is a complete trust.

I have so many pictures and stories to go with them that maybe I will have to do a book on that sometime. Keep looking up, don't look down. God's artwork is amazing!

On occasion while doing the angel of God prayer, angels have appeared in the sky. If you want to live a better life this truly is the way. This is God Our Father's book, not mine. I am just the other. If you do what it is in this book for advice and live it, get ready to count your blessings because you will receive many. The blessings will override any trials or crosses that you carry, and all things will be done through God. We have a very short journey on this earth no matter how long we live. Life is short, but Heaven is forever! Let's help one another to make sure we get there! Would love all of you and to be together in eternity! May God bless you and love and prayers always! Love to all of you reading this.

Linda Fay Black

God wanted me to write a book for him about the truth. I listen to our Father when he asks me something. Whether

237

it be picking up a Pepsi can and throwing it away or writing a book. When asked, I said yes to doing it. He let me know that this is not my book, it is his. I am just the writer. He wants the truth to be known and how to live our lives in peace. He wishes to help all of us and knows that we all need it. This book will change your views and life and complete all that you need throughout our journey here. Father loves all of us so very much and wishes to help aid us. This book is from God, not me. He used me to be his helper to get it accomplished but it is his book to all of you. I can't wait for your life to unravel and experience the gift of truth! God will give many blessings to whomever shall take a moment and read his book.

Love Father—who used me to be the author. I am just a seed, he is everything and all you need! It really is the truth!

Truth

Printed in the USA
CPSIA information can be obtained
at www.ICGtesting.com
LVHW012016121223
766210LV00005B/47

9 781645 362210